SCHIRMER PERFORMANCE EDITIONS

HAL LEONARD PI

M000113320

BEETHOVEN

PIANO SONATAS
VOLUME I
Nos. 1–15

Edited by Robert Taub

The commentary on the sonatas has been excerpted and abridged from *Playing the Beethoven Piano Sonatas* by Robert Taub, published by Amadeus Press, distributed by Hal Leonard Corporation.

On the cover:
Woman at Dawn
by Caspar David Friedrich
(1774–1840)
Museum Folkwang, Essen, West Germany/The Bridgeman Art Library Nationality

ISBN 978-1-4234-0392-0

G. SCHIRMER, *Inc.*

7777 W. Bluemound Rd. P.O. Box 13819 Milwaukee, WI 53213

Copyright © 2010 by G. Schirmer, Inc. (ASCAP) New York, NY
International Copyright Secured. All Rights Reserved.

Warning: Unauthorized reproduction of this publication is prohibited by Federal law and subject to criminal prosecution.

www.schirmer.com
www.halleonard.com

CONTENTS

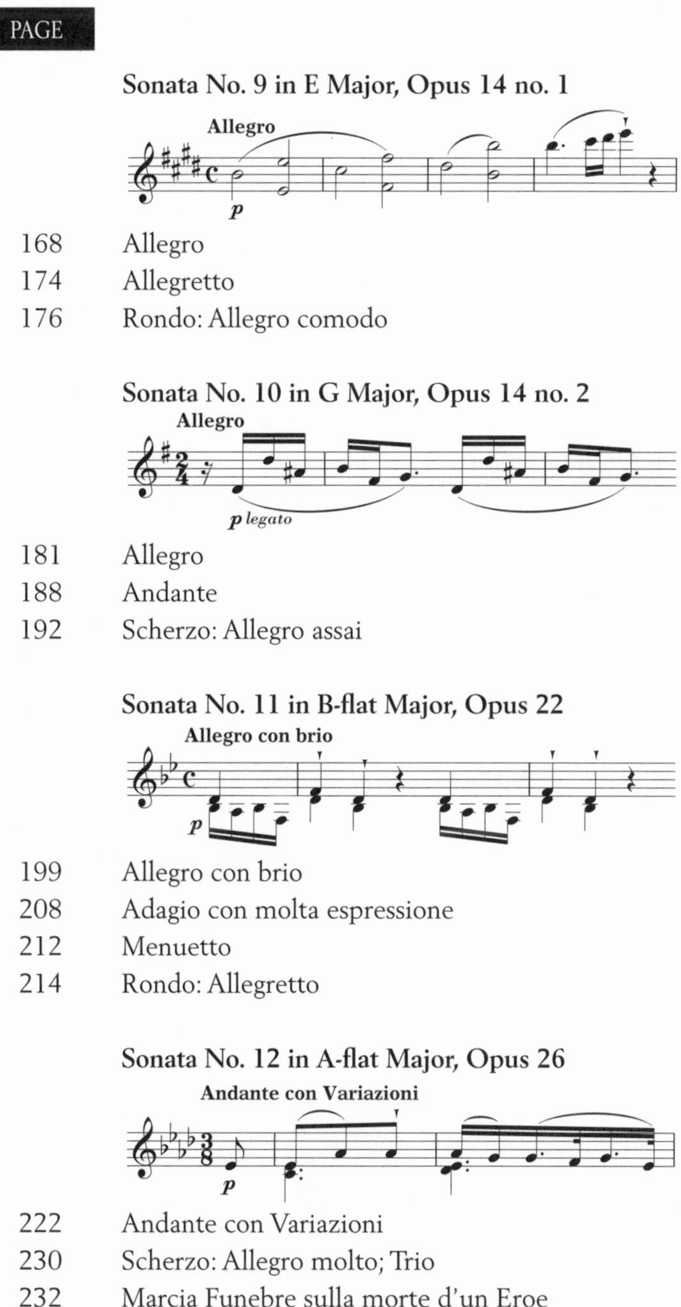

PAGE

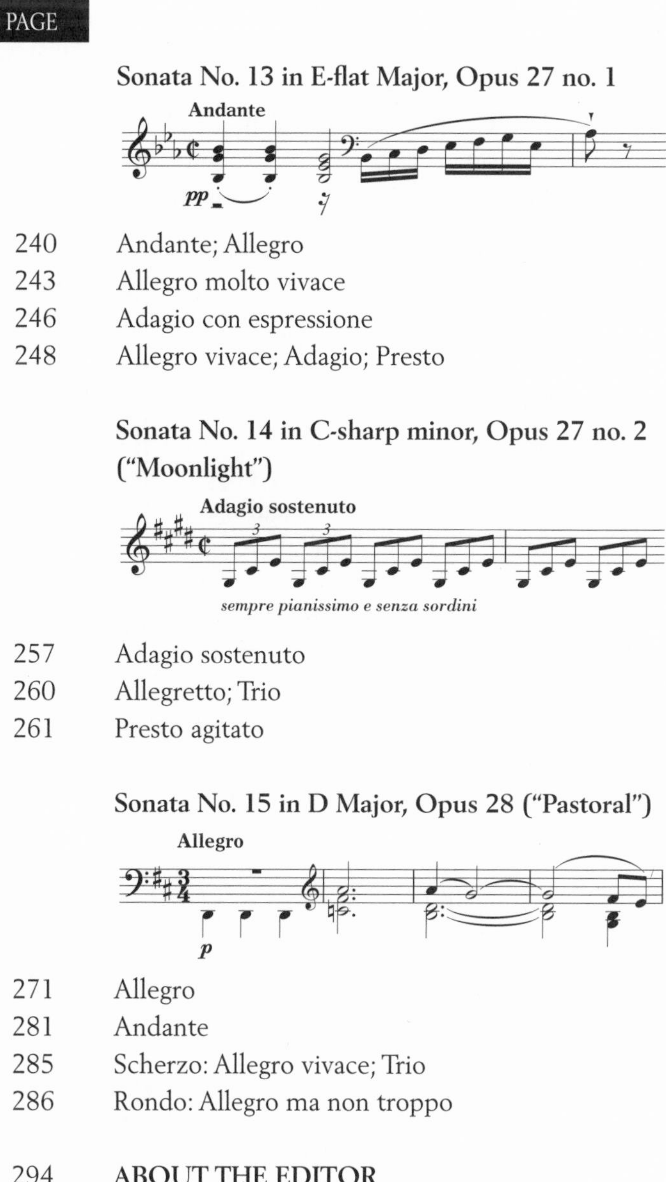

PAGE

HISTORICAL NOTES

Ludwig van Beethoven (1770–1827)

THE PIANO SONATAS

In 1816, Beethoven wrote to his friend and admirer Carl Czerny: "You must forgive a composer who would rather hear his work just as he had written it, however beautifully you played it otherwise." Having lost patience with Czerny's excessive interpolations in the piano part of a performance of Beethoven's Quintet for Piano and Winds, Op. 16, Beethoven also addressed the envelope sarcastically to "Herr von Zerni, celebrated virtuoso." On all levels, Beethoven meant what he wrote.

As a composer who bridged the gulf between court and private patronage on one hand (the world of Bach, Handel, Haydn, and Mozart) and on the other hand earning a living based substantially on sales of printed works and/or public performances (the world of Brahms), Beethoven was one of the first composers to become almost obsessively concerned with the accuracy of his published scores. He often bemoaned the seeming unending streams of mistakes. "Fehler—fehler!—Sie sind selbst ein einziger Fehler" ("Mistakes—mistakes!—You yourselves are a unique mistake") he wrote to the august publishing firm of Breitkopf und Härtel in 1811.

It is not surprising, therefore, that toward the end of his life Beethoven twice (1822 and again in 1825) begged his publishers C.F. Peters and Schott to bring out a comprehensive complete edition of his works over which Beethoven himself would have editorial control, and would thus be able to ensure accuracy in all dimensions—notes, pedaling and fingering, expressive notations (dynamics, slurs), and articulations, and even movement headings. This never happened.

Beethoven was also obsessive about his musical sketches that he kept with him throughout his mature life. Desk sketchbooks, pocket sketchbooks: thousands of pages reveal his innermost compositional musings, his labored processes of creativity, the ideas that he abandoned, and the many others—often jumbled together—that he crafted through dint of extraordinary determination, single-minded purpose, and the inspiration of genius into works that endure all exigencies of time and place. In the autograph scores that Beethoven then sent on to publishers, further layers of the creative processes abound. But even these scores might not be the final word in a particular work; there are instances in which Beethoven made textual changes, additions, or deletions by way of letters to publishers, corrections to proofs, and/or post-publication changes to first editions.

We can appreciate the unique qualities of the Beethoven piano sonatas on many different levels. Beethoven's own relationship with these works was fundamentally different from his relationship to his works of other genres. The early sonatas served as vehicles for the young Beethoven as both composer and pianist forging his path in Vienna, the musical capital of Europe at that time. Throughout his compositional lifetime, even when he no longer performed publicly as a pianist, Beethoven used his thirty-two piano sonatas as crucibles for all manner of musical ideas, many of which he later re-crafted—often in a distilled or more rarefied manner—in the sixteen string quartets and the nine symphonies.

The pianoforte was evolving at an enormous rate during the last years of the eighteenth century extending through the first several decades of the nineteenth. As a leading pianist and musical figure of his day, Beethoven was in the vanguard of this technological development. He was not content to confine his often explosive playing to the smaller sonorous capabilities of the instruments he had on hand; similarly, his compositions demanded more from the pianofortes of the day—greater depth of sonority, more subtle levels of keyboard finesse and control, and increased registral range. These sonatas themselves pushed forward further development and technical innovation from the piano manufacturers.

Motivating many of the sonatas are elements of extraordinary—even revolutionary—musical experimentation extending into domains of form, harmonic development, use of the instrument, and demands placed upon the performer, the piano, and the audience. However, the evolution of these works is not a simple straight line.

I believe that the usual chronological groupings of "early," "middle," and "late" are too superficial for Beethoven's piano sonatas. Since he composed more piano sonatas than substantial works of any other single genre (except songs) and the period of composition of the piano sonatas extends virtually throughout Beethoven's entire creative life, I prefer chronological groupings derived from more specific biographical and stylistic considerations. I delve into greater depth on this and other aspects of the sonatas in my book *Playing the Beethoven Piano Sonatas* (Amadeus Press).

1795–1800: Sonatas Op. 2 no. 1, Op. 2 no. 2, Op. 2 no. 3, Op. 7, Op. 10 no. 1, Op. 10 no. 2, Op. 10 no. 3, Op. 13, Op. 14 no. 1, Op. 14 no. 2, Op. 22, Op. 49 no. 1, Op. 49 no. 2

1800–1802: Sonatas Op. 26, Op. 27 no. 1, Op. 27 no. 2, Op. 28, Op. 31 no. 1, Op. 31 no. 2, Op. 31 no. 3

1804: Sonatas Op. 53, Op. 54, Op. 57

1809: Sonatas Op. 78, Op. 79, Op. 81a

1816–1822: Sonatas Op. 90, Op. 101, Op. 106, Op. 109, Op. 110, Op. 111

From 1804 (post-Heiligenstadt) forward, there were no more multiple sonata opus numbers; each work was assigned its own opus. Beethoven no longer played in public, and his relationship with the sonatas changed subtly.

—Robert Taub

PERFORMANCE NOTES

For the preparation of this edition, I have consulted autograph scores, first editions, and sketchbooks whenever possible. (Complete autograph scores of only twelve of the piano sonatas—plus the autograph of only the first movement of Sonata Op. 81a—have survived.) I have also read Beethoven's letters with particular attention to his many remarks concerning performances of his day and the lists of specific changes/corrections that he sent to publishers. We all know—as did Beethoven—that musical notation is imperfect, but it is the closest representation we have to the artistic ideal of a composer. We strive to represent that ideal as thoroughly and accurately as possible.

Tempo

My recordings of these sonatas are available as companions to the two published volumes. I have also included my suggestions for tempo (metronome markings) for each sonata, at the beginning of each movement.

Fingering

I have included Beethoven's own fingering suggestions. His fingerings—intended not only for himself (in earlier sonatas) but primarily for successive generations of pianists—often reveal intensely musical intentions in their shaping of musical contour and molding of the hands to create specific musical textures. I have added my own fingering suggestions, all of which are aimed at creating meaningful musical constructs. As a general guide, I believe in minimizing hand motions as much as possible, and therefore many of my fingering suggestions are based on the pianist's hands proceeding in a straight line as long as musically viable and physically practicable. I also believe that the pianist can develop senses of tactile feeling for specific musical patterns.

Pedaling

I have also included Beethoven's pedal markings in this edition. These indications are integral parts of the musical fabric. However, since most often no pedal indication is offered, whenever necessary one should use the right pedal—sparingly and subtly—to help achieve legato playing as well as to enhance sonorities.

Ornamentation

My suggestions regarding ornamental turns concern the notion of keeping the contour smooth while providing an expressive musical gesture with an increased sense of forward direction. The actual starting note of a turn depends on the specific context: if it is preceded by the same note (as in Sonata Op. 10 no. 2, second movement, m. 42), then I would suggest that the turn is four notes, starting on the upper neighbor: upper neighbor, main note, lower neighbor, main note.

Sonata in F Major, Op. 10 no. 2:
second movement, m. 42, r.h.

However, if the turn is preceded by another note (as in Sonata Op. 10 no. 2, first movement, m. 38), then the turn could be five notes in total, starting on the main note: main note, upper neighbor, main note, lower neighbor, main note.

Sonata in F Major, Op. 10 no. 2:
first movement, m. 38, r.h.

Whenever Beethoven included an afterbeat (Nachschlag) for a trill, I have included it as well. When he did not, I have not added any.

Footnotes

Footnotes within the musical score offer contextual explanations and alternatives based on earlier representations of the music (first editions, autograph scores) that Beethoven had seen and corrected. In areas where specific markings are visible only in the autograph score, I explain the reasons and context for my choices of musical representation. Other footnotes are intended to clarify ways of playing specific ornaments.

Notes on the Sonatas[1]

SONATA NO. 1 IN F MINOR, OPUS 2 NO. 1 (1795)

In autumn 1795, the twenty-five-year-old Beethoven played the three Sonatas Op. 2 for his former composition teacher Haydn, to whom they are dedicated, at a Friday morning concert at Prince Lichnowsky's (a great supporter of music in Vienna). Beethoven considered the three sonatas of Op. 2 illustrative of his ideals as a composer and pianist and worthy of publication, and they furthered his introduction into Viennese musical society.

The challenges of playing this piece begin with the first note of the **Allegro**. It has no phrase marking; it is not staccato, but neither is it legato, for it is not slurred to the following staccato notes. I play the opening C with more weight than the following staccato notes, but I make sure not to connect it in phrasing by separating it with a slight air space from the following F.

The use of dynamics is immediately striking—the first six measures build from *p* to *ff*, then fall away back to *p* by m. 8. The opening figure increases in intensity and corresponding sharpness of touch as it rises, and each time the turn at the end is played, it is also at a higher dynamic level.

Although the second theme is simply an inversion of the first, the entire musical feeling is different. The top line is now as legato as possible while the undulating left hand playing only E-flats now gives a feeling of instability. The *con espressione* marking that begins the ending of the exposition implies a slight lessening of the tempo. The C-flats here give a hint of E-flat minor; a weighty touch can help emphasize this subtlety.

Initially the dynamic in the development is *piano*. The crescendos, *fp* and *sf* markings, and the increased pace of harmonic change and increased registral range of the second theme (played in the bass beginning in m. 67) all generate greater intensity in this area of the piece. A clear sound, gradual increase of tension in the touch, and spare pedaling will allow the tensile strength of the counterpoint to prevail.

In observing the repeat sign for the second part of this movement, I maintain the tempo, saving the fermata over the last rest for the conclusion of the movement.

The first sixteen measures of the **Adagio** of Op. 2 no. 1 are a transcription of the second movement of a piano quartet (WoO 36) Beethoven had composed some ten years earlier. Clarity of lines is important in this movement. Textures are spare, and the general quality of sound is *dolce* (rather than the more syrupy *espressivo*).

The graceful **Menuetto** and the **Trio** remain in F (minor and major respectively). Both break with the pattern of eight-bar phrases, again postponing local cadences and thereby creating feelings of suspension. I believe that the dynamic contrasts in the second part of the Menuetto are sudden contrasts, not to be anticipated by crescendos or decrescendos. This is not merely a question of making one hand more prominent than the other but has more to do with qualities of voicing and sound, achieved by subtleties of touch and pedaling.

Beethoven used the term **Prestissimo** sparingly. When he wrote it, he meant it. Hence, the last movement of this sonata is played very fast indeed. The ubiquitous triplets at the beginning of this movement and the concentrated juxtaposition of dynamic extremes create an underpinning of urgency.

The middle section of this movement, marked *sempre piano e dolce*, provides an extraordinary contrast to the intensity of the first section. The music at the beginning of this area is structurally a transmutation of the music at the beginning of the sonata; the repeated left-hand chords and the rising right-hand arpeggio that begins the now aria-like theme hark back—perhaps subliminally for the listener but certainly consciously for the composer—to the material of the first movement.

Beethoven included repeat signs for both parts of the last movement, which allows the opportunity to play (and hear) the repetition of the music slightly differently from the way we hear it the first time through.

1 Excerpted from *Playing the Beethoven Piano Sonatas* by Robert Taub
edited and abridged by Susanne Sheston
© 2002 by Robert Taub
Published by Amadeus Press
Used by permission.

SONATA NO. 2 IN A MAJOR, OPUS 2 NO. 2 (1795)

Sonata in A major, Op. 2 no. 2, is a gentle and graceful work, the most playful of the three in this opus.

From the beginning of the opening **Allegro vivace**, I use a light touch and clear articulation (well-rounded fingers!) as the opening interval (A–E) is manipulated to motivate the entire first theme area. The swirling counterpoint gives the impression of frisky new voices constantly being added, and the tempo can be quick enough to give a sense of urgent direction to the ascending lines, for the sixteenth and thirty-second note figures are not difficult to play fast. However, the *espressivo* marking in mm. 58–59 implies a lessening of tempo as well as a deeper quality of sound and touch.

Contrasts in touch help convey the differences in feeling between the first and second theme areas. Whereas the lines of the first theme area are tossed back and forth playfully between the two hands, the second theme, a single melodic line in the treble area, has a heavier, singing tone. The left hand accompanies and can play more lightly than the right, increasing in intensity as it ascends. Since I take Beethoven's fingering indications in the cascading octave triplet arpeggios (mm. 84–89) to indicate a smoothness of line as well as a display of brilliant virtuosity, I make sure not to rush the tempo in these measures and in those immediately preceding

The characterization of the slow movement of Sonata Op. 2 no. 2—**Largo appassionato**—is highly individual. Usually passion is associated with faster music, but here the slow and dignified music is of an ardor sincere and ingenuous. The detached bass is the line with the greatest amount of motion. The long, sustained right-hand chords in this movement stand in great contrast to the rapid motion of the top line of the first movement, and playing them with a weighty touch and a sense of solemnity helps create the quiet but impassioned mood. Throughout the movement, whenever the opening music is heard, the right hand is marked *tenuto sempre*, the left, *staccato sempre*. Yet even within these indications, there are enormous contrasts of touch and sound: consider the *fortissimo* D minor area in m. 58 and the *pianissimo* recurrence of D major in a higher octave in m. 68. The prolongation of the final cadence is again analogous to a long goodbye in Italian opera; a little extra emphasis on the low left-hand A's, prolonging the six-four chord, heightens this feeling.

The reworking of the A–E interval that so motivated the first movement also helps to make the **Scherzo: Allegretto** frolicsome. Now it is heard only in arpeggiated fragments, ascending, played almost in an off-the-cuff manner. The longer lines of the Trio provide contrast, as does the minor mode, and the *sforzando* markings highlight the entrances of new implied voices.

In the **Rondo: Grazioso**, the same A–E interval is expanded over a two-and-a-half-octave span. It would have been far easier for Beethoven to write simply two eighth notes at the end of the first beat of m. 2 (and in analogous places), but instead, the sixteenth rest following the sixteenth note implies a lift, a breath, helping significantly to establish the graceful disposition of the movement. Whenever the theme recurs, the arpeggio is slightly different, but a sixteenth rest always follows.

Contrasting with the smoothness and elegance of the first part of the Rondo, the middle section starts *fortissimo*, with staccato chromatic lines accompanying forceful dotted rhythms. The music drives forward; even when the lines are legato, *pianissimo*, and back in a major mode (m. 80 on) there is an underlying restlessness that is relieved only with the return in m. 100 of the main thematic A–E interval, now fully extended over three-and-a-half octaves! Quick changes of mood, touch, and tone color are needed in the coda of this movement (beginning in m. 148) to create a microcosm in which the principal nature of each theme resurfaces.

SONATA NO. 3 IN C MAJOR, OPUS 2 NO. 3 (1795)

From the start of the **Allegro con brio**, Sonata Op. 2 no. 3 is a virtuosic work. Even the careful articulation of the registrally restrained first measure—making sure the staccato chords of the fourth beat are indeed light and separated from the previous legato sixteenth notes, all within *piano*—is enervating as the music seems to effervesce beneath its sparkling surface. As the main motive is tossed back and forth between the registers and hands, I maintain the general level of the *piano* so that the *fortissimo* in m. 13 is a complete and utter surprise. In the virtuosic sixteenth-note passages that follow, the touch is strong indeed, but also transparent, with pedal used only lightly.

Beethoven was careful about the dynamics at the beginning of the development. The left-hand chords are only *forte*, but the right-hand sixteenth notes start *fortissimo* (m. 97). Immediately, the syncopated element of the second theme is seized upon in minor key harmonies and combined with the most salient elements of the first theme. The *sforzandos* in both are important, for these offbeat accents increase dramatic tension.

A large-scale coda, including a quasi-improvisatory cadenza, balances the development area. Although one might expect a cadenza in a piano concerto, it is most unusual in a piano sonata, but such was the scale of Beethoven's conception of this movement. Therefore, I take quite a bit of time with the fermata at the beginning of m. 232 and begin the ensuing right-hand figure somewhat under tempo. Even though there are no indications for articulation in this cadenza, I maintain the well-established groupings of four legato sixteenth notes followed by two staccato eighth notes since the cadenza is built entirely from this motive, and gradually increase the tempo to the fermata on the trill. The tremolando flourish that concludes the movement harks back also to the first theme, and although it begins *fortissimo*, I drop in dynamic immediately only to become louder again as the line rises and softer as it falls. The final two chords end most emphatically.

The **Adagio** is in the rather surprising key of the mediant, E major. The tempo can be slow, stately, and steady throughout, without rushing even when the harmonic motion slows (mm. 41–42), so that the reentry of the first theme (m. 43) is seamless. When this theme returns yet again (m. 67) following the only *fortissimo* outburst of the movement, the touch is thinner and more concentrated for it is in a higher register.

Contributing to the playful character of the **Scherzo: Allegro** is the delightful way the themes enter and accrue, all in a light staccato touch. This fugal opening, which becomes simply canonic, necessitates clarity of voicing and careful attention to the dynamics, specifically the *forte subito* markings in m. 13, m. 27, and m. 54.

Although there is no dynamic marking at the beginning of the Trio, I start it *forte*, for the A minor tonality along with the virtuosic waves of triplets over the left-hand octaves implies a strong, dramatic character. Clarity here is also important, and therefore I pedal only lightly, sometimes touching the pedal for only the first beat of each measure, not allowing too much sound to accrue. The Trio ends *fortissimo* so that the return of the *piano* Scherzo is a stark contrast.

A consideration when playing the **Allegro assai** is maintaining a unified tempo throughout, regardless of contrasting character of the themes. The tempo of the movement is therefore planned by the maximum speed allowing clarity of the second theme; although the first theme can be played faster, I believe that unity of pacing is more important.

In the body of this movement, the main theme is always stated by the right hand in the middle and upper register, *piano*, with the right wrist relaxed. The coda, however, starts with a *fortissimo* declaration of this theme by the left hand in the tenor register, under a right-hand trill on high C. It is now the left wrist's turn to stay relaxed. Beethoven suggested fingerings for the virtuoso chordal passage beginning in m. 269, which I find helpful and use.

SONATA NO. 4 IN E-FLAT MAJOR, OPUS 7 (1797)

Sonata Op. 7 contains a profusion of musical ideas. A basic and striking aspect of the piece is the overt presence of repeated notes in the first, second, and fourth movements and their more subtle presence in the trio of the third movement. These repeated notes help create the impression of underlying motion even within a static harmony, lending qualities of both tension and ebullience to the work.

Allegro molto e con brio implies a brisk tempo, but the unit of pulse should remain the eighth note to ensure a pulse of six per measure. This will imbue the music with more palpable feelings of inner drive and direction than would be possible by playing the movement in two. Because of the length of the opening chords and slightly falling contour within each two-bar unit, the musical shape is an implied diminuendo from m. 1 to m. 2 and again from m. 3 to m. 4.

The rising and falling contour and the increasing sweep of the legato lines that follow give the impression of moving forward, although they are still in strict tempo. I like to make a big contrast between the stentorian *fortissimo* measures (mm. 25 and 29) and the questioning *pianissimo* bars that follow (mm. 26 and 30). Each rhetorical outburst is a harmonic surprise; I stress the bass register and play deeply into the keys with plenty of pedal. The higher chords are within the same harmony; I voice slightly toward the top, with a light staccato touch, with small amounts of pedal only in the driest of acoustical situations.

Contrasting with everything that came before is the choralelike texture of the second theme (m. 59 on). The hands are still, quiet, and as smooth as possible. In the close of the exposition, the rapid sixteenth-note tremolandos in the right hand create hints of minor harmonies for the first time in this work, and as they need to be clear the pulse of six should be maintained. I find that the basic tempo of the movement really derives from the maximum speed of this area.

Like the first movement, the **Largo, con gran espressione** begins with four chords, but their dynamic shaping contrasts with that of the four which opened the Allegro. Voicing of the chords becomes important, especially in m. 7 with the introduction of a specific alto line and a poignant A-flat appoggiatura. I take a little time to set up the *sforzando* and to infuse the surprise of its presence with dramatic tension.

In the second theme area, the *sempre tenuto* marking for the right hand contrasts with the staccato left hand. This simultaneous opposition of touches is not easily achieved. It is tempting to use pedal to help connect the right-hand chords, but this would interfere with the detached left-hand notes. I try to use a touch in the right hand that produces a deep, singing tone, and I change fingers as often as necessary on the top notes of the chords to achieve a sense of smoothness. If pedal is used, it should be used only sparingly.

I like to begin the **Allegro** minuet with a very sweet tone, softly, giving the impression of emerging gradually from the great stillness of the slow movement's end. It is important to give the measure of rest (m. 69) its full due—how unusual it is to have a full measure of silence in the midst of a piece! This measure keeps us in suspense, awaiting a harmonic resolution that arrives in the form of solo B-flats, repeated notes once again.

The willowy and flowing character of the **Rondo: Poco allegretto e grazioso** contrasts from the brilliance of the first movement, the spaciousness of the second, and the alternating amiability and agitation of the third. I use a very singing tone in the right hand for the first part of the Rondo theme and a more rhetorical contrast of touches in the left hand for the second part (m. 16 on). The very ending of this movement is simple and elegant—no virtuosity, no drama, just reverberation of the final cadence.

SONATA NO. 5 IN C MINOR, OPUS 10 NO. 1 (1796–98)

After having established himself with the four-movement sonatas of Op. 2 and Op. 7, Beethoven compressed the sonata to three movements in Op. 10 nos. 1 and 2. The first of these sonatas is dramatic and concise; the *forte* beginning of Sonata Op. 10 no. 1 makes audiences sit up in their chairs. The rhetorical style—propulsive dotted rhythms, abrupt dynamic changes, and C minor setting—is intense, passionate, and stormy.

The opening flourish of the **Allegro molto e con brio** exemplifies the unambiguous manner in which harmonies are presented, as well as spanning the compass of the treble register of the pianoforte as it then existed. The tempo can be brisk, although for metrical strength and clarity, it is important to maintain a pulse of three beats per measure rather than a pulse of one. I like to make the most of the dynamic contrasts; one *pianissimo* marking, two *piano*, three *forte*, and four *fortissimo* markings concentrated within only the first thirty-two measures reveal an intense and fiery spirit.

The long, lyrical lines of the second theme contrast with the short motivic fragments of the first, but rhetorical qualities—particularly large registral spans, such as the two-and-a-half-octave leap in m. 71—are still ubiquitous. The movement could end at the penultimate cadence (m. 281) in the coda: the home key of C minor has been reestablished and the recapitulation is complete. Therefore, I elongate the rests in that measure ever so slightly, giving the impression that the movement is indeed finished. As a result of this slight delay, the *fortissimo* final cadence becomes a surprise, consistent with the high drama throughout.

The registral leaps and juxtapositions of dynamics of the first movement are smoothed in the **Adagio molto**. I use as singing a tone as possible, with gentle but firm pressure on the keys. The quality of sound in the *forte* areas (for example, m. 17 on) is different from the *forte* areas of the first movement: the sound here is deeper and rounder. The music reaches an expressive apex in mm. 98–99 as the theme is abstracted into octaves in the top line with full harmonies and syncopation to support—here it is nice to expand slightly in time as well as in dynamics.

The **Finale: Prestissimo** begins in an urgent whisper, as the terse first theme develops gradually over three statements of the initial rhythmic motive. After a long fermata, the more melodic second theme of the Prestissimo also accrues over three statements of its own motivic kernel. Registral leaps and dynamic extremes (*ff* to *p*) abound. Tension builds throughout this movement as Beethoven eschews any cadence on the home key (C minor). When it is finally attained in m. 100, the music begins to feel more like an ending. Since it stays in this key for only two measures, and to heighten the surprise of the entrance of the bass A-flat in m. 102, I wait slightly after the last chord of m. 101. The restatement of the second theme in the unlikely key of D-flat major is quasi-improvisatory, with flexibility of pulse; here Beethoven has specified both ritard and calando.

The flourish of a dominant arpeggio (briefly reminiscent of those of the first movement) leads into the coda, which concludes dramatically but softly with three descending statements of the opening motive. There is no ritard, only a decrescendo; the pacing of the music remains steady, and the fermata over the eighth rest ensures the silence necessary for the drama to resolve.

SONATA NO. 6 IN F MAJOR, OPUS 10 NO. 2 (1796–98)

In Sonata Op. 10 no. 2, declamation gives way to questioning, and stormy weightiness to gentle playfulness.

In the **Allegro**, careful articulation of the sixteenth-note triplets (as in m. 1), separating them from the staccato quarter note that follows—as Beethoven notated—contributes to the clarity of texture and the frolicsome nature of this figure. It also allows for a marked contrast with the longer legato arched line that follows. Careful grading of dynamics also adds to the rich mosaic of thematic adventures, which reach their virtuosic zenith with the crossing of hands for the right-hand trills in the bass and then the treble registers.

The development area is rhythmically motivated by sixteenth-note triplets (first heard in m. 1). A steady pulse is of the utmost importance throughout the shifting harmonies. This pulse is abandoned with the fermata in m. 117, which leaves us hanging—in registral extremes—awaiting the recapitulation, but as a musical joke in the "wrong" key (D major). The "correct" key (F major) is reestablished, but not before a tangential hint at G minor.

In keeping with the light-hearted character of this work, there is no true slow movement. Instead, the middle movement is an **Allegretto** (minuet and trio), but it is in a minor key (F minor), songful and searching in mood. The tempo needs to be spacious enough to allow for both clarity of voicing and for tension in the syncopated areas. The opening of this movement—initially empty octave unisons—is the longest legato line of the sonata. I use a touch that creates a sound that is as smooth, bell-like, and hollow as possible, moderating only when harmonies subtly accrue beginning in m. 5—fingers well curved, wrists flexible, light pedal leading into a deeper, weightier sensation. In playing the opening of the trio, I voice the portato chords slightly to the top but still maintain the warmth of the lower register in this new D-flat major texture.

The **Presto** of this sonata is lithe and jaunty. Although it is much easier to slur the groups of four sixteenth notes into the following eighth note, Beethoven marked them as separated, and playing them as such gives the music more of its characteristic lift. The *forte* heralding the change of key at the beginning of the development area comes as a surprise. This section of the piece has the most rapid rate of harmonic change, and clarity in voicing of the mock fugato gives the impression that the music is swirling all around us. In m. 87 on, although the only dynamic indication is *fortissimo*, the counterpoint to the theme—the running sixteenth notes—can be shaped by their contour, falling in dynamic level slightly as they descend, rising in level as they ascend. This concept applies to the overall shape of the thematic line as well. Since both sections of this movement are repeated and the last four measures are marked *fortissimo*, I save a little strength for the last time through, making the last cadence the most conclusive.

SONATA NO. 7 IN D MAJOR, OPUS 10 NO. 3 (1796–98)

The energetic opening line of Sonata Op. 10 no. 3—complete with fermata at the end—augurs a substantial work. It is the longest and most weighty sonata of Op. 10 and is the first Beethoven sonata with a slow movement in a minor key—no small matter, since slow movements by Beethoven as well as by his classical predecessors Haydn and Mozart were generally in a major mode.

Clear articulation of the sonata's opening line of the **Presto** is of utmost importance, not only for the beginning, but also because this line recurs in many different ways, with contrasting articulation, throughout the entire work. (The first four notes are taken up and reinterpreted immediately, legato, beginning in mm. 4–5.) As the opening line rises and increases in intensity, it is natural to increase the dynamics slightly. I also make the staccato notes a bit sharper as the line ascends. The real crescendo should be saved, though, until m. 18, where the line is syncopated and its trajectory leads beyond the A of m. 4 to F-sharp, *fortissimo*. Frequently throughout the exposition, as fragments or elements of the main theme reassert themselves, often starting from a gentle, *piano* texture, careful pedaling is necessary to ensure signature staccato characteristics.

As the development begins by changing the familiar four-note motive from major to minor (m. 124–125), I would warn against taking any special time for the F-natural. Doing so would be too obvious; I would suggest instead a subtle change in touch from confident and assertive (though *pianissimo*) to questioning and introspective, as if wondering where the music could go from here.

In the slow movement—**Largo e mesto** (slow and sad)—the descending minor second of the initial theme (D–C-sharp) is transformed into a monument of expression. The meter and pulse is six beats to a measure, the chords are sonorous, and the top line sings mournfully above. I like to make sure that the rests in the right hand beginning in m. 36 are felt; they are sighs, gasps. Even though the bell-like tolling continues in the bass, if the rests are not heard interrupting the top line, they lose their significance. Rests assume an even greater significance before the main theme recurs, when they are prolonged significantly, increasing tension silently (mm. 41–42).

Menuetto: Allegro. Believing the tempo of a trio is basically the same as for the surrounding scherzo or minuet sections, I take the cue for the speed of the next movement from the triplets of the Trio. They are the fastest surface motion. As an emotional foil to the inner turbulence of the Largo e mesto, the Menuetto is simple and uncluttered; careful voicing and phrasing keep it elegant. The Trio is more boisterous, with its crossing of hands and a *fortissimo* outburst in the middle.

The **Rondo: Allegro** opens with a three-note motive, a transposition of the fifth, sixth, and seventh pitches of the Presto's main theme. Just as the first four notes of this figure play such a consuming role in the first movement, so do the next three notes now serve to motivate and indeed permeate the Rondo. Instead of being staccato, they are now legato, but the staccato octaves from the opening theme of the Presto return in mm. 10–12. This is a playful movement, with many changes of direction and mood.

In m. 92 on, both the three-note and the four-note motives are played consecutively again, but the order is "wrong"—the three-note motive is first. Hence, the *sforzando* at the start of each four-note group is important to accentuate. When the right hand emerges from the D octave in m. 106 to play its nearly chromatic scale up and down the keyboard, the inverted three-note motive in the left hand should predominate even in *piano*; the right should not obscure the left. The last note, the low D, is only a quarter note, not longer; the fermata over the last rest ensures that the piece concludes in silence.

SONATA NO. 8 IN C MINOR, OPUS 13 ("Pathétique") (1798–99)

Beethoven himself designated the sobriquet "Pathétique," indicating that he fully intended for others to appreciate the dramatic content of Sonata Op. 13. Like his other two piano sonatas in C minor (Op. 10 no. 1 and Op. 111), the "Pathétique" is infused with extraordinary intensity.

The first marking of the **Grave** of Op. 13 is *fp*: what does it mean? How is it played? The idea is for the chord to be heard *forte* initially, then rapidly dying down to *piano*. This is fundamentally different from an accent within a *piano* context and from the *sforzando* marking first encountered here in m. 3. To achieve an effective *fp*, the pianist simply depresses the keys rapidly, creating the *forte*, then immediately allows them to rise so that the sound is damped almost instantaneously. Depressing the keys immediately once again so that the dampers rise quickly allows the strings to continue to vibrate but now with considerably less energy, *piano*. All this takes only a small fraction of a second but sets the stage for the drama that unfolds throughout the piece.

The tempo of the Grave is slow enough so that the sixty-fourth-note groupings are clear but not so slow as to be ponderous. The Allegro molto e con brio enters without interruption, and here, since the harmonic motion is basically slow, I play at the fastest tempo that allows for the bass tremolandos—which add mightily to the overall tension of the movement—to be transparent with only subtle pedaling. The touch on the staccato half notes (m. 15) is light, and the chords are separated but not sharply detached. I do not see any reason to slow down for the second theme (m. 51 on) but rather use a more singing tone and legato qualities of touch. I play all the mordents (m. 57 on) starting with the main note, on the beat.

In the development area, crescendos that were withheld from the ascending right-hand line in the exposition are present and give the impression that the line is pushing forward even though the tempo remains steady. For the first time (beginning in m. 150), the left hand has the melodic fragments under right-hand tremolandos, which should remain vibrant as they descend chromatically. Notably, the recapitulation does not include music from the opening Grave, but the coda does.

After the contrasts of tempo of the first movement and its interruptions of phrases, its staccato notes, and its inner tension; the long, singing phrases of the **Adagio cantabile** appear as welcome comfort. The movement is unabashedly lyrical with a three-tiered texture. Each line requires a different quality of sound, a different touch—flat fingers playing lightly for an accompaniment touch; slightly heavier, more rounded fingers for a singing tone.

Each of the two episodes concentrates on a different musical character. The stillness of the repeated bass and questioning character of the top line of the first episode contrast with the introspective, conversant qualities of the second. When the theme returns for the last time (m. 51) the accompaniment continues the triplet motion begun in the second episode, but it is important not to push the tempo ahead at this point and to maintain the repose of the character of the theme.

An interpretive decision for the **Rondo: Allegro** concerns its fundamental character. Is it tempestuous and headlong like the first movement, or is it more restrained, more held back? I believe the latter is the case. Although this movement is alla breve, I play it less fast than the first, at a speed that allows the lyricism of the top line to be felt in all its poignancy.

To preserve the tempo and for inner strength where the triplets begin (m. 33), I find a pulse of four beats per bar—rather than simply two—is helpful. Openness of tone—even within a dynamic of *piano*—is generally the rule in major key areas such as m. 44, in contrast to the soft intensity of the C minor theme.

SONATA NO. 9 IN E MAJOR, OPUS 14 NO.1 (1798–99)

The two Sonatas Op. 14 are both rather intimate works of three movements. Although each begins with a sonata-form Allegro, neither sonata has a true slow movement. The middle movement of Op. 14 no. 1 is an Allegretto minuet and trio, and the last is a gently paced Rondo: Allegro comodo. Sonata Op. 14 no. 2 enchants us with a theme with three variations (Andante) as its second movement. Usually a scherzo is found as a middle movement in a large-scale sonata, but this sonata concludes with a Scherzo: Allegro assai. In keeping with the smaller formal scope of both Sonatas Op. 14, their main themes in all movements are more registrally confined than are the themes of many preceding Beethoven sonatas. Accordingly, the Op. 14 sonatas are more immediately "singable."

The lyrical qualities of Op. 14 no. 1 are apparent from the outset of the **Allegro** as the right hand plays its ascending melodic line accompanied by the pulsating left-hand chords. I like to voice these chords slightly to the top, for the right hand compresses the ascending line made by these notes (B–C-sharp–D-sharp–E) in m. 4 to conclude the first phrase. The initially simple four-bar phrase structure is extended beginning in m. 15 as the left hand rises chromatically, and the right hand increases in intensity with the crescendo to *forte* and the staccato half-note chords. I consider the staccato markings as referring to the quality of touch and sound—sharper touch, octaves almost plucked off the keys—rather than to the duration of the sound, for the fact that these are half notes (and not eighth notes) indicates that the sound can be held by the pedal, creating a more pointed and resonant sonority.

In the development, changing fingers frequently on the top notes of the octaves can help establish the legato sound. Perhaps a very slight slowing down toward the end of the decrescendo in mm. 89–90 adds to the harmonic preparation for the return to the home key of E major, but there is no reason to take time before the surprise *forte* entrance of the recapitulation. Careful pedaling at the end of the movement will help ensure that too much sound does not accumulate, that the dynamic level remains *pianissimo*, and that the movement ends gently.

The duet in octaves between the two hands at the beginning of the **Allegretto** establishes this movement as essentially a lyrical one, and by the direction of the note stems Beethoven has indicated that the voicing of the chords is of great importance. The crescendo in m. 62 over an empty two-octave span is a challenge. I use the pedal to ensure a blending of the two E's and I try to make the second grow out of the sonority of the first, even though that sonority is less on the third beat than on the first. The crescendo marking guards against making the second E softer, which would otherwise naturally be the predilection, and thus helps establish the *piano* marking in the following measure to be a *piano subito*. This *piano subito* establishes an immediate contrast between the two sections—the E minor minuet and the C major trio that follows. The short coda combines the feelings—and qualities of touch—of both the minuet and the trio to conclude this songful movement.

The tempo of the last movement is designated as **Rondo: Allegro comodo**—a comfortable allegro—implying a speed that is not too fast. As the initial right-hand octaves remain in the same register as the music heard at the beginning of the sonata, the descending left-hand triplets need to be well articulated so that the changing harmonies of the right-hand octaves can be heard. The second theme (m. 21) begins with a solo right-hand line that is initially harmonically ambiguous, as was the second theme of the first movement. However, instead of playing with the increasing intensity of an ascending chromatic line, I play the second theme here with questioning playfulness. Seriousness of mood is reserved for the development section; the virtuosic right-hand triplets are accentuated slightly on the first of each group to hint at an implied line. The dynamics of this line—although within the general level of *forte*—can be shaped with the rising and falling contours of the music. With parallel treatment of the left-hand octaves, this creates the area of greatest intensity in the entire work. The lilting syncopations in the coda—more thematic abstraction—are a further element of playfulness.

SONATA NO. 10 IN G MAJOR, OPUS 14 NO. 2 (1798–99)

The **Allegro** of Sonata Op. 14 no. 2 begins gently, creating a melody from nothing, always moving subtly forward by small harmonic changes. Even the left hand is gentle and mellifluous: no crashing chords, no full chords—in fact, no chords of any sort. This is the first of Beethoven's sonatas to begin in this way. When a texture involving chords finally does appear (m. 26 beginning of the second theme), the feeling is of a duet in the top line, rather than chordal accompaniment.

With the addition of the B-flat to the thematic melody in m. 64, the beginning of the development is plaintive but still gentle. This melody is further transformed in the beginning of m. 81, when a *forte* octave appears for the first time, heralding the thematic line in the bass. The tension is heightened even further by the right hand playing sixteenth-note triplets against the duple sixteenths in the left, and by the sharp staccato sixteenth notes beginning in m. 84. Whatever slight rhythmic flexibility there might have been with this line at the start of the development is now gone; the two against three, the left-hand staccato marking, the *forte* dynamic all imply a strict pulse.

The chordal texture of the **Andante** certainly makes up for any lack of simultaneities in the first. This theme and three variations are charmingly inventive; more than rhythmic, harmonic, or registral transformations of the theme, it is the accompaniment of the main line—the counterpoint—that is varied as the music unfolds. Right before the last variation, Beethoven holds us in suspense—as if we are backpedaling—as the dominant harmony is repeated for four measures (mm. 61–64). Pianistic touch becomes lighter and the pulse slightly relaxed as the right-hand chords are subtly voiced to the inside chromatic descent. Time is elongated once again in the final three measures, as the pace of the theme is augmented twofold. This helps set up the final chord, but its *fortissimo* dynamic—a huge joke that jolts everyone out of complacency—is always a surprise.

Playfulness continues in the following **Scherzo: Allegro assai**. Although this movement is in triple meter, the main theme starts with three consecutive duplets, and rhythmic emphasis frequently shifts away from the downbeat. The resulting lilt lends the music a metrical unpredictability. In mm. 10 and 12, for example, I avoid any hint of an accent on the downbeat; the trajectory of the line is to the top right-hand C on the second beat.

Even the trio is not immune to musical joking, for the four measures of decrescendo (mm. 105–108) are an extension of the fourth consecutive eight-bar phrase, mocking and satirical in a good-natured way. The *sforzandos* in the coda make even more explicit the antics of the metrical instability of the main theme, and the *pianissimo* ending in the deep bass completes the escapade.

SONATA NO. 11 IN B-FLAT MAJOR, OPUS 22 (1800)

Sonata Op. 22, a wonderful piece, is played less frequently than many, perhaps because the gentle last movement does not excite audiences to a fevered pitch.

The **Allegro con brio** of Op. 22 is full of life, with a high level of enthusiasm that seems to bubble just barely beneath the surface. I prefer a quick, spirited tempo, and make the opening measures very light, with the right-hand sixteenth notes well articulated. This approach propels the listener forward to the main line beginning in m. 4, which is the only true melody of the entire exposition. When the left hand has the theme in mm. 11–12, curved fingers and clear articulation will help counteract any impulse to rush. I consider the *sforzandos* in mm. 16, 18, and 20 to be sharp impulses within a general context of *piano*, with a further drop to *pianissimo* for the start of the second theme. Although the dominant is reached as early as m. 38, which could mark the end of the exposition, further embellishments and repeated arrivals on the dominant continue for another thirty measures. Leading up to each of these dominant arrivals, I like to give the impression by preparing the cadence that the section is coming to an end, but then play through the surprising continuations maintaining a trajectory all the way to m. 68.

In the development, I drop from repeated levels of *fortissimo* to levels of *piano* when elements of the first theme return in different keys (mm. 83, 87, and 91). In m. 105, in ever lower registers, the left hand plays the line that closed the exposition until reaching the lowest note on Beethoven's piano (low F, m. 116). I hold the fermata in m. 127 long enough to preserve the inherent tension of the *pianissimo* dominant chord, but not so long that the sound dies away completely.

From the outset, the **Adagio con molta espressione** is full of operatic lyricism. I play the opening left-hand chords with a pure accompaniment touch—flat fingers gently sweeping off the keys. In the canon that follows the surprising move to G major in m. 31, I like to establish terraces of voices, keeping each one independent in dynamics from the others. To create the illusion of a crescendo on the sustained top and bottom B-flats in both mm. 43 and 44, I make a slight swell with the inner voices but then allow them to drop again as the last two eighth notes of the top and bottom voices continue the crescendo. When the main theme returns in m. 47, I allow the embellished areas to be relaxed in pacing, in the nature of a true singing, breathing line. At the end of the movement, I wait before the penultimate chord to make sure that the last two chords will indeed be very soft.

In the beginning of the **Menuetto**, I make a distinct difference between the singing top line and the accompaniment. This difference blurs in mm. 9 and 13, though, where I make the hands more equal, possibly even favoring the left hand the second time through. I also play the initial eight-bar phrase differently in its first and second appearances: the first time arises out of silence and is softer. Keeping a steady tempo in the overtly dramatic Minore trio will allow the offbeat *sforzando* right-hand chords to sound more menacing than a pacing that rushes.

I have found that the most successful performances of the **Rondo: Allegretto** are those that do not try to make this movement into something it isn't, but rather accept the music for what it is—gentle and graceful—and revel in it. The tempo is not fast; it is leisurely. Even when octaves enter in the right hand in m. 9, they are not virtuosic, but rather simply a fuller, more open, singing line. Throughout, harmonies are firmly grounded.

In the coda, I make sure to keep an eighth-note pulse within the seemingly long quarter notes with which it starts (mm. 182–183) in order not to rush. The left-hand fingers are firm and articulate the thirty-second notes smoothly.

SONATA NO. 12 IN A-FLAT MAJOR, OPUS 26 (1800–01)

A challenge in playing Sonata Op. 26 is deciding how to highlight the new and different moods of each of the five variations in the **Andante con Variazioni**. While all retain the same melodic and harmonic outline of the theme, each reflects a different aspect of pianism and distributes salient melodic features in increasingly abstract ways. One facet of the theme that is subsequently exploited in different ways in the ensuing variations is the specific use of register for a melody or melodic fragment.

At the beginning of the theme, each hand is voiced to the top since the main line is in unison between them. However, in the B area (mm. 16/17–26), the hands alternate in importance. The *sforzandos* in the left hand and its single line imply that the left-hand line comes more to the fore, with the right hand coming out more for the second part of this phrase. The first variation follows the same general scheme, with more playful and extensive use of register, particularly for the A phrases. Therefore the first variation is played with more dynamic shadings than the theme.

In the second variation the melodic line is abstracted in the bass only, with equal weighting for each note of the octave. When the right-hand octaves move chromatically for the first four measures of this phrase (mm. 16–19) I bring out the top line more than the bass. In the second section of this phrase, the left hand plays out more, for it has the main line. This weighting of the hands is the opposite from the theme and the first variation.

The central variation is a somber modulation into the tonic minor. Although the right hand has the main melodic line, the left-hand *sforzandos* provide strong metrical and harmonic anchor points, and I take a little time for the first of these (m. 9), especially within the dynamic of *piano*. I play all the right-hand two-note phrases of the fourth variation as legato as possible, contrasting with the sharp staccato chords in the left hand. With the last variation I use more pedal as a thicker texture is established. Careful voicing to the inside, while keeping the top measured trill as light as possible beginning in m. 9, means that the thumb and second finger of the right hand are weighted more heavily than is the rest of the hand.

The biting *sforzando* on the first downbeat of the next movement is played with vigor, even within a *piano* context. In the second part of the **Scherzo: Allegro molto**, I bring out the theme, first in the left hand (m. 44) and then in the right (m. 52), the first time through. Upon the repeat I bring out the corresponding counterpoint a bit more but still keep the theme as primary.

The **Marcia Funebre** is a stylized funeral march for the death of a hypothetical hero (a style not unpopular of the time), with dotted rhythms characteristic of the genre. However, the enharmonic changes by which Beethoven opens new expressive vistas are extraordinary. To the listener, the B minor harmony in m. 9 is a surprise, so I drop slightly in dynamic level and take a little time at the first beat. Tremolandos in the middle section of this movement are stylized drum rolls, and as sonority builds by virtue of crescendos and keeping the pedal down, it is important for the tempo to remain very steady.

The **Allegro** is basically a gentle piece. The only area of dramatic tension follows the second statement of the theme and recalls the tremolandos of the funeral march as it delves into minor harmonies. Although sixteenth-note patterns continue, the touch is different here; to produce a more focused sound, one that is more direct and less relaxed, the fingers are a bit more curved, and I play more on the tips, with a bit more weight.

SONATA NO. 13 IN E-FLAT MAJOR, OPUS 27 NO. 1 (1800–01)

The Op. 27 sonatas continue to expand musical perceptions and the notions of what a sonata can be. Beethoven designated each of the two Op. 27 sonatas as *quasi una fantasia*, implying departures from expected structures and indicating a sense of temporal continuity throughout each work. He wrote, between the first and second movements, *Attacca subito l'Allegro* (begin the Allegro at once), adding parallel *attacca* indications following the second and third movements as well. The only heavy double bar comes at the very end of the piece.

The pacing of Op. 27 no. 1 was unusual by contemporaneous musical expectations. Rather than beginning with a lively Allegro first movement, the opening is **Andante**. The harmonic rhythm is leisurely: only two harmonies—the tonic and the dominant—are heard for the first minute or so. Because of this relaxed pacing, subtleties of voicing and dynamics are particularly important. When finally in m. 13 a surprise C major harmony is heard, the *pianissimo* dynamic draws in the listener. When C major recurs as the allegro interruption beginning in m. 36, clean articulation—only slight pedaling—of the arpeggios along with the considerable contrast engendered by the *forte* and *piano* dynamics can help maximize the visceral excitement. In this fantasy nothing is wasted, for just as the surprise of C major in m. 13 led to the entire C major Allegro middle section beginning in m. 36, the C minor of m. 57 is more fully developed in the Allegro molto vivace second movement that follows. The final chord of the movement, *pianissimo*, *senza sordino*, is a hollow sound, which is filled in by the sudden and unbroken start of the next movement.

A characteristic of the **Allegro molto vivace** is the rapid pulse of three, which leads first to playful syncopations within each measure in the trio and next, when the opening music of the scherzo recurs, to syncopations at a more intense level within the beat. A tempo that is too fast and that leads to a feeling of one beat per measure—rather than three beats per measure—will not allow the full impact of the syncopations to be felt.

There is a distinct singing line throughout the **Adagio con espressione**. Voicing, therefore, is important, as are subtleties in the left-hand touch. The entire Adagio is closely aligned to the key of A-flat major, so the establishment of the dominant harmony in the last three measures is crucial to the arrival back in the home key of E-flat major at the beginning of the Allegro vivace.

At the beginning of the **Allegro vivace**, which again enters without a break in sound, the left hand should be well articulated in order for the right to be heard distinctly, and the right pedal used only sparingly. When the main theme is played in chords (without the sixteenth-note accompaniment) in mm. 25–35, enough time should be taken before the *piano* echoes so that the contrasts between the dynamic levels are maintained and the *piano* chords—even the first of each group—stand out. This is part of the vitality of the movement.

At the end of the movement we are left suspended on the dominant harmony, where the music of the Adagio recurs, no longer in A-flat major, but rather in the home key of E-flat major. A fantasy involves the recurrence of musical elements, but even though this recurrence surprises a listener, the home key lends feelings of reminiscence and, in a sense, the beginning of the end. Only the first phrase of the Adagio is played, and as the cadence at the end of this phrase is first repeated and then postponed, the feeling of improvisation—of spinning out the line—deepens. The final flourish in the coda is brilliant and virtuosic, and the last two chords impart a special air of finality, for not only are they *fortissimo*, they are also the only V–I cadence at the end of a movement in this work.

SONATA NO. 14 IN C-SHARP MINOR, OPUS 27 NO. 2 ("Moonlight") (1801)

Although the first movement of this sonata may be among Beethoven's best-known piano compositions, the complete sonata, and particularly the anguished drama of the last movement, offers such a compelling artistic experience that I would hope that anyone who has played only the first movement would also become immersed in the rest of the work.

The character of the **Adagio sostenuto** is striking, with its gently veiled sonorities shifting subtly, wisps of melodic fragments floating above. The alla breve time signature implies a pulse of two beats per measure, even within Beethoven's designation of Adagio sostenuto, which guards against the music becoming lugubrious.

At the beginning of the movement, Beethoven included two indications for *senza sordini* (without dampers): *Si deve suonare tutto questo pezzo delicatissimamente e senza sordini* and *sempre pianissimo e senza sordini* (this whole piece ought to be played with the utmost delicacy and without dampers—and then—always very soft and without dampers). While I depress the pedal only slightly, just enough to raise the dampers off the strings to allow them to vibrate freely, the character of this movement requires the pedal to be changed discretely to avoid creating harmonic sludge. The *senza sordini* indication pertains to the entire first movement as a general approach to the quality of sound, similar to the initial *sempre pianissimo* indication.

The three-part texture that pervades this movement suggests different qualities of touch and sound for each different voice. The bass octaves are soft but deep, the undulating triplets are smooth and played with an accompaniment touch (flat, light fingers, not pressing too deeply into the keys), and the top line, although *pianissimo*, sings forth in a plaintive voice. In this Sonata *quasi una fantasia*, there is no second theme in the first movement—such were expectations stretched. The triplet accompaniment assumes a more melodic role and can be shaped accordingly as it is developed beginning in m. 32 on. Tension increases as new harmonies are explored, the bass remaining insistently on the G-sharp octave (the dominant) and the top line temporarily abandoned in favor of the searching qualities of the triplets.

In the short coda the portentous dotted rhythm is heard for the first time in the bass (but exclusively on G-sharps) as it exchanges registral placement with the triplets. The movement ends as quietly as it began. Beethoven wrote *Attacca subito il seguente*—an element of fantasia heard also in Op. 27 no. 1—and the second movement begins without any break in sound.

Despite the quicker pacing of the **Allegretto**, the mood is wistful and the textures delicate. The smooth lines of the Allegretto give way to *sforzando* syncopations in the trio, a contrasting spot of good humor in this sonata. I like to voice the left-hand chords in mm. 45–48 first to the tenor and then to the bass upon the repeat, giving a slight weight to the chromatic lines. Although the Allegretto ends with a rest, I would think it very much in keeping with *quasi fantasia* to begin the third movement almost right away. Once again, an enharmonic change (this time from D-flat major back to C-sharp minor) is the pivot point.

This **Presto agitato** is the most extended of the three, and is the most overt dramatic center of the piece. I prefer a genuinely fast tempo; although the harmonic motion is not particularly rapid, finally the surface motion can be, and a feeling of agitation is generated from both speed and clarity. From the start, a three-part texture analogous to that of the first movement is established: the bass line is distinct, the upwardly climbing sixteenth-note figures are a general middle area, and the top register is reached with the punctuated eighth-note chords—*sforzando*, staccato, in pedal.

There are two fermatas, both over bare G-sharps, which is the dominant pitch and is hence fraught with expectations of resolution—one in m. 14 and the other in the parallel place in the recapitulation (m. 115). I hold these fermatas a long time. By creating feelings of suspense, seemingly spontaneously, they are crucial to the fantasia element, as is the four-measure cadenza-like passage in mm. 163–166, just four measures into the extended coda.

SONATA NO. 15 IN D MAJOR, OPUS 28 ("Pastoral") (1801)

When I play Sonata Op. 28 in concert on a piano that is unfamiliar to me, I take some time to accustom myself to the subtle ways in which the low D key repeats (m. 1) and how the hammer is voiced. I check the degree of aftertouch to determine whether the key needs to be allowed to rise all the way to the top before it is played again in order to create a smooth, gently pulsating texture. I also experiment with both pedals. I use the left pedal if the D's hammer is a bit hard, to try to obtain a full but quiet quality of sound. The degree to which the pedal is depressed also depends on the voicing of the hammer, as well as on the acoustics of the hall. Most often, I do not change the right pedal until the downbeat of m. 3. I depress it lightly, just enough to allow the strings to vibrate freely.

From the start of the **Allegro**, I think it is important to establish a pulse of three beats per measure, rather than playing with only one beat to the bar. Throughout the first theme area, I give a little extra weight to the stepwise movements of the bass while playing the right hand as legato as possible, particularly in the octaves. The phrase in mm. 71–76, right before the start of the second theme (m. 77 on), is again elongated. I allow the music to grow slightly in time here as well as in volume; as the crescendo reaches its apex in m. 76, I also make a slight ritard before the *piano subito* in m. 77. Just as the top and bottom lines of the first theme are smooth, I maintain a legato touch throughout the second theme area.

The character of the development area becomes increasingly agitated as thematic phrases are broken down into smaller and smaller motivic units. As the last two bars of each phrase are repeated in close succession (m. 199 on), touch becomes more intense even though the dynamic initially drops to *piano*, and tension increases palpably. In m. 227, the harmony of F-sharp major is attained and the music drops suddenly to *piano*. I am careful to keep that level of dynamic even when the hands spread out to accommodate the increased registral span a few measures later.

To establish the tempo of the **Andante**, I find it helpful to consider the speed of the thirty-second notes beginning in m. 47. This abstraction of the theme is melodic and can't be too fast; on the other hand, neither can it be so slow as to be lugubrious and funereal. I try to keep the right hand playing smoothly over the bass staccato notes, and maintain an eighth-note pulse within the 2/4 meter.

Improvisatory qualities enter the arena with the fermatas in mm. 86 and 88, the second of which I hold longer than the first. I play the right-hand B-flat in m. 94 clearly enough so that it sustains all the way to the A of m. 95, and then the ensuing two-note groupings of mm. 96–97 with enough diminuendo within each group so that, along with the rests, they sound almost like whispered sobs.

The playful **Scherzo: Allegro vivace** is motivated by the motion of repeated notes but reinterpreted in different registers and settings. A subtle two-part texture is maintained by voicing the top note of each descending octave slightly more than the bottom note; I make sure to separate the last slurred eighth note (first beat of m. 5 on) from the second beat, just as written, even though it is considerably easier to connect the eighth notes to the quarter note on the second beat. The overall tempo of this movement is determined by the speed of this section. If the Scherzo starts too fast, then the Trio will be either unplayable or artificially slower if the pianist slows down in order to play accurately.

In the **Rondo: Allegro ma non troppo**, the pulse is six eighth notes to a measure, and as in the first movement, the low D serves as anchor point throughout the first theme. Playing the right hand as if the music is initially off in the distance contributes to the bucolic character of the music. I start in strict tempo, ending the first two right-hand entrances as quietly and seemingly deftly as they began. In mm. 9–11, playing as the markings indicate imparts a sense of going to the third beat and coming away from it, avoiding a more clichéd accentuation on the fourth beat. In m. 17, I try to maintain a steady pulse here to guard against pushing the tempo; even when *forte* is reached in m. 26, the character is strong but gentle, not aggressive.

In the final part of the coda—più allegro quasi presto—I use a light touch for the left hand and a relaxed wrist, keeping the hand close to the keyboard, and close, well-articulated fingers in the right hand. Rather than resorting to playing in two just because the tempo is faster, I still try to maintain the pulse of six per bar to inject the music with as much excitement and virtuosity as possible.

Final Thoughts

Beethoven's sonatas—as individual works, or taken together as a complete cycle—are pieces that we can listen to, learn, play, put away, relearn, and perform again over and over—with only increasing joy, involvement, and meaning. For those of you looking at the musical score as you follow a recording, welcome. For those playing these pieces for the first time, I invite you to become involved. And for those returning to these sonatas after learning them previously—or comparing this edition to any other—I invite you to roll up your sleeves and start playing, for there is always more to do. The expressive universe conjured up by the Beethoven piano sonatas is unprecedented, and unequalled.

—*Robert Taub*

References

For sources consulted in researching this edition, please see the Bibliography in *Playing the Beethoven Piano Sonatas*, by Robert Taub, published by Amadeus Press (Hal Leonard Corporation).

Dedicated to Joseph Haydn

Sonata in F minor

Opus 2 no. 1
Composed in 1795

Allegro (𝅗𝅥 = 116)

1.

a) The fingering in italics is Beethoven's. b) short appoggiatura, played before the beat c) 

Copyright © 2010 by G. Schirmer, Inc. (ASCAP) New York, NY
International Copyright Secured. All Rights Reserved.

con espress.

d) The Artaria first edition (1796) and Simrock (1798) include repetition signs for the second part of this movement.

e) D-flat, not D-natural f)

89
decresc.
pp
95
pp
cresc.
100
f
sf
sf
105
sf
sf
ff
p
110
p
115
p

120
125
130
cresc.
135
140
con espress.
146

Adagio (♪ = 72)
dolce
p
sf
pp
rinf.
j) as in g)
G-sharp also in Artaria;
in Lischke, simply ∾

18
21
sf
sf
24
sf
sf
26
pp
28
sfp
1)
30
sfp
sf
pp
sf
p
1)

33
36
m)
38
pp
40
42
44
sf
sf
pp
m)

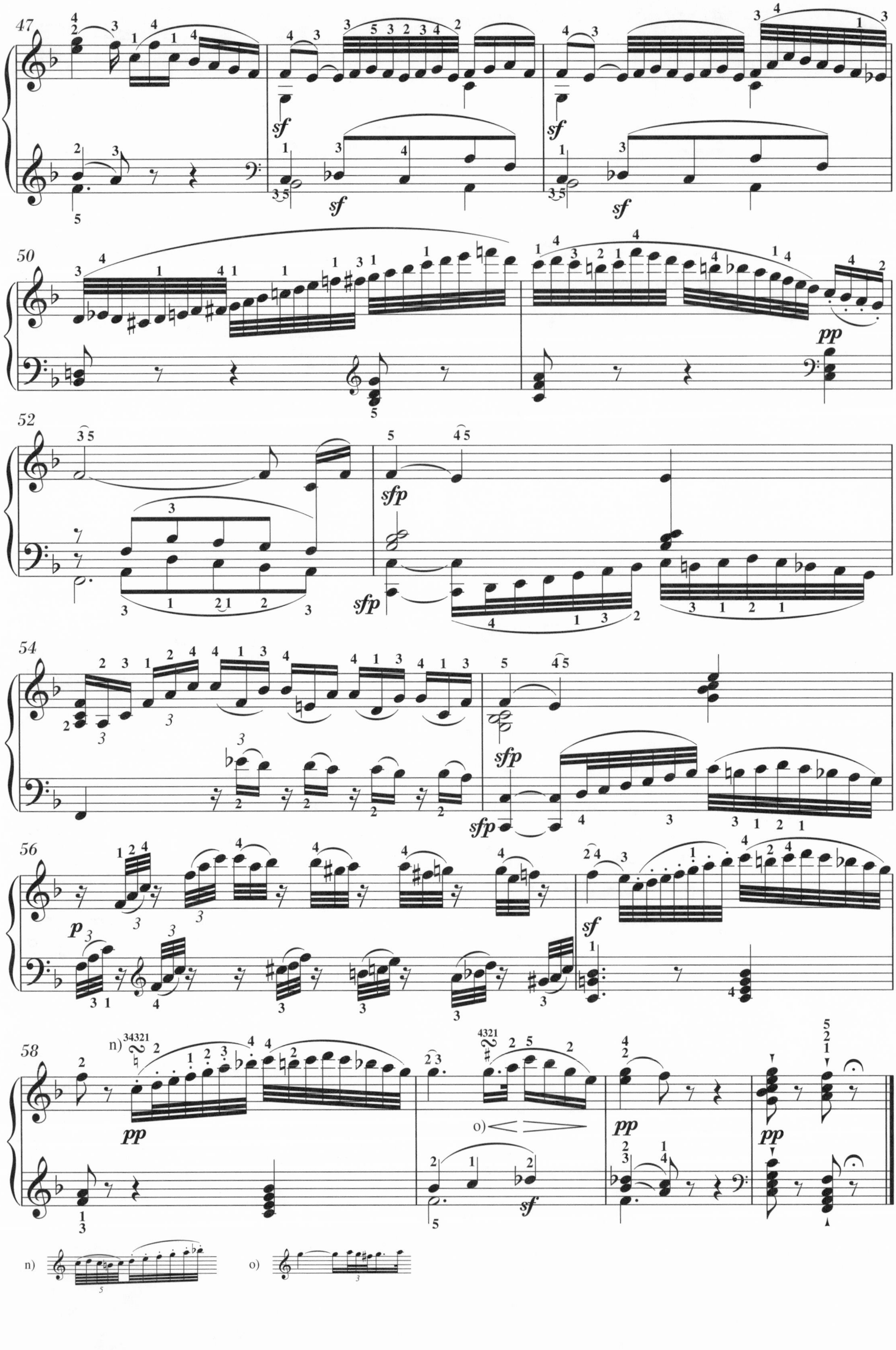
47
50
52
54
56
58
sf
sfp
pp
p
n)
o)

MENUETTO

Allegretto (♩ = 144)

p) Played as a short appoggiatura: in contrast to the written-out long appoggiatura in mm. 22 and 23.

40/41
TRIO
p
47
54
60
ff
p
pp
p
67
Menuetto D.C.

Prestissimo (𝅗𝅥 = 108)

q) without tail

83
tr
89
rinf.
rinf.
96
tr
tr
102
rinf.
rinf.
109
pp
sf
pp
114
sf
pp

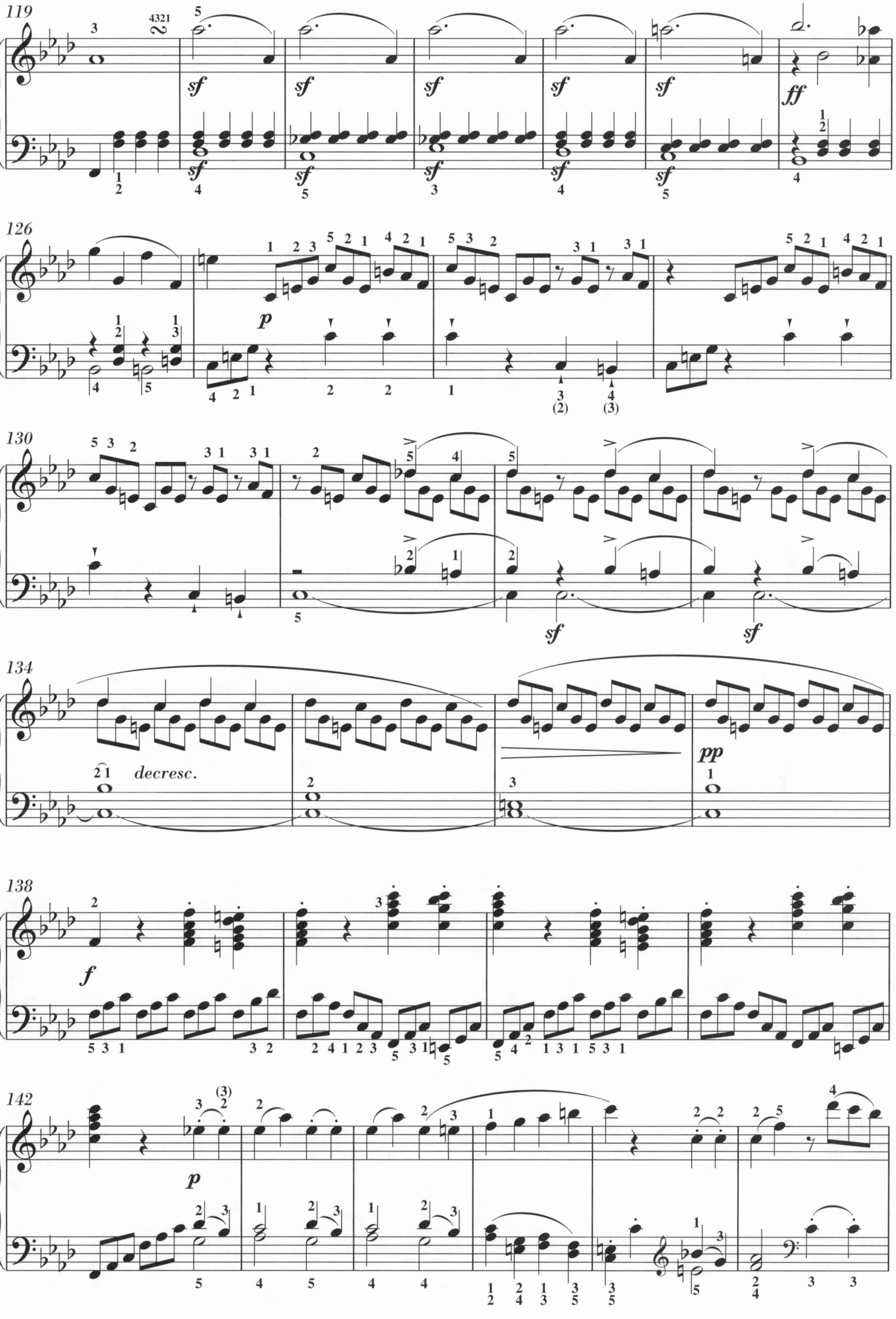
119
126
130
134
decresc.
138
142

148
tr
fp
p
153
f
p
f
f
157
ff
sf
161
165
169

173
p
177
181
p
185
189
f
193
ff

Dedicated to Joseph Haydn

Sonata in A Major

Opus 2 no. 2
Composed in 1795

a) The fingering in italics is Beethoven's.

Copyright © 2010 by G. Schirmer, Inc. (ASCAP) New York, NY
International Copyright Secured. All Rights Reserved.

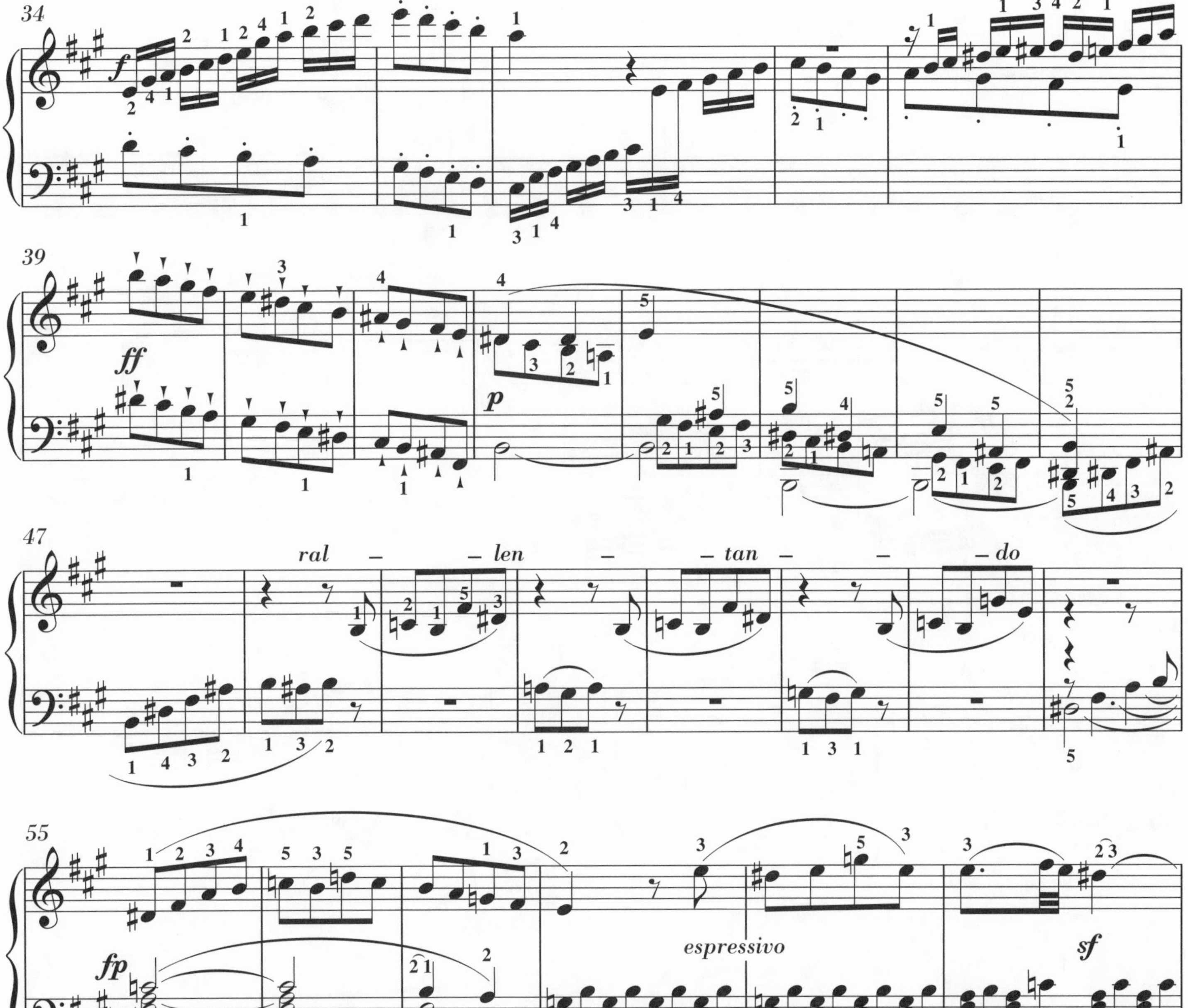

ral – – len – – tan – – – do

espressivo

b) The first edition (Artaria, 1796) has ~; the Berlin edition (Lischke, 1797), ~ with ♮.

c) In Artaria, ♯♯∽; in Lischke, ♯∽. d) In Artaria and Lischke, ♯∽. e) Beethoven's fingering here (and in parallel passages), although challenging, is purposefully integral to the musical fabric, creating a smooth musical line as a transition back to the opening tempo from the subtly slightly slower second theme. An often-cited alternative method of playing this passage—using the LH to play the first of each three-note group—is superficially easier, but often creates a pointillistic bravura display that countermands the musical value.

f) LH over RH g) After Artaria and Lischke, other editions print E-flat instead of G.

h) In m. 203, Artaria and Lischke have four G-sharps in the upper voice. Later editions have what is printed here. This change, which parallels m. 207, may be assumed to be the result of a correction to the first edition made by Beethoven.

218
pp calando
f
227
f
p
fp
236
pp
pp
245
ff
sf
253
sf
sf
257
ff
p

i) In Artaria and Lischke, ~♮. j) In Artaria and Lischke, ~♯. k) In Artaria and Lischke, ~♯.

1) In both first editions, only E–B in LH.

m) For the sake of "languid expression" (C.P.E. Bach), the turn may begin on the second eighth note. n) The trill begins with the principal note.

o) p) Notation of LH follows Artaria. Lischke prints and some more recent editions print

tenuto
staccato

cresc.
ff
tenuto sempre
staccato sempre
sf
p
sfp
pp legato
tenuto sempre
staccato sempre
pp

q) Expressive short appoggiatura:

r) *ff*, as in Artasia; in Lischke, the *ff* is one measure later.

RONDO
Grazioso (♩ = 120)

23
26
sf
29
sf
32
sf
35
38
pp

staccato sempre
sf
pp
ff

59
sf
62
65
1.
2.
67
stacc.
ff
sf
70
sf
73
(sf)

(sf)
sf
sf
legato
pp
sf
sf
sf
sf
ff
(sf)
(sf)
dim.
pp

94
97
100
103
106
109

112

115

dolce

118

121

124

sf

127

sf

sf

pp
mf
sf

151
154
157
161
164
167
f
p
f
f
sf
sf
ff
sf
sf
sf
sf
sf
sf
sf
sf
sf
sf
sf
sf
p
sf

170
decresc.
173
pp
175
178
sfp
181
sf
184
f
p

Dedicated to Joseph Haydn

Sonata in C Major

Opus 2 no. 3
Composed in 1795

a) The fingering in italics is Beethoven's.

Copyright © 2010 by G. Schirmer, Inc. (ASCAP) New York, NY
International Copyright Secured. All Rights Reserved.

b) Release thumb on B; hold for ♪. duration in pedal

p
dolce
f
c)
d) without tail

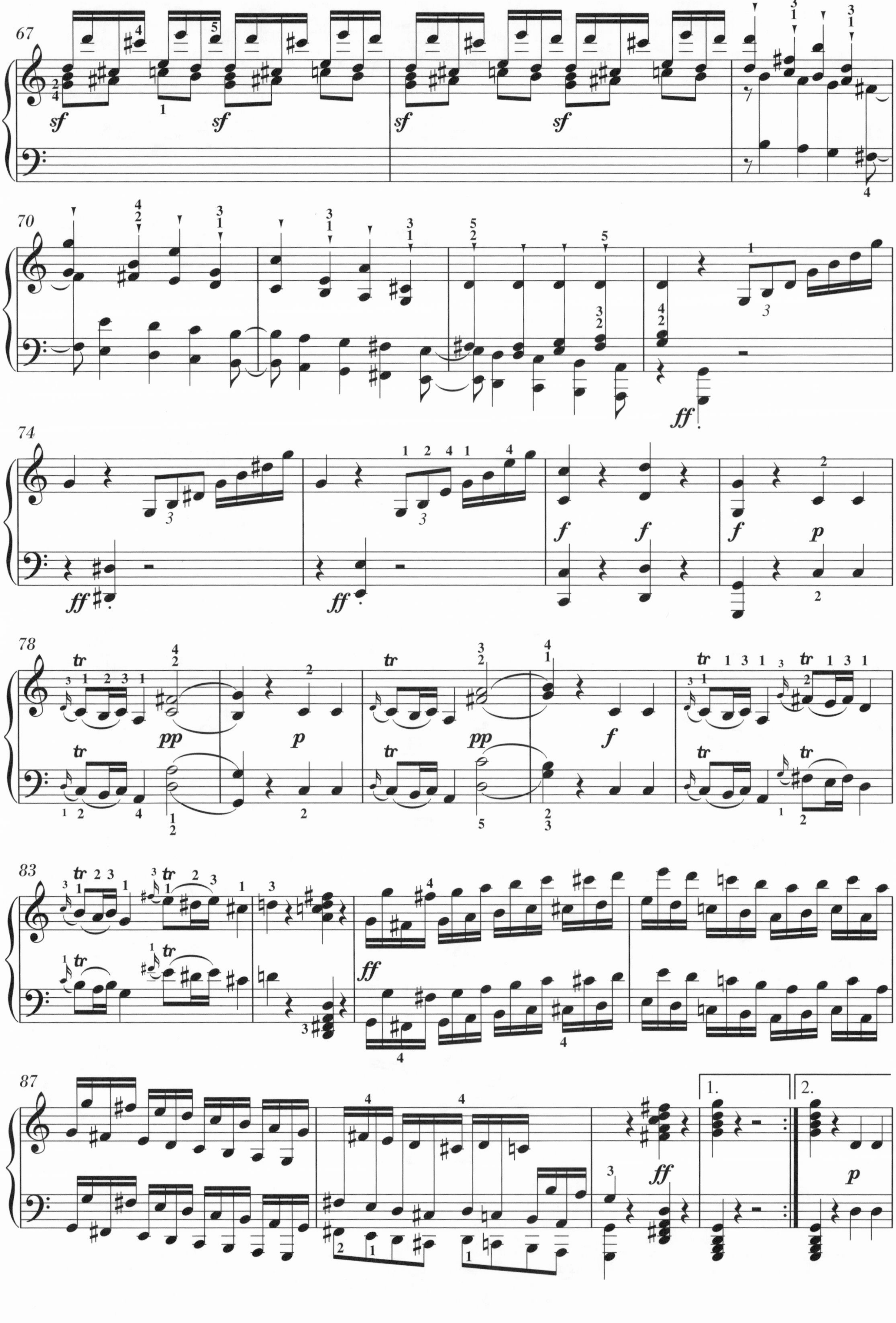
67
sf
sf
sf
sf
70
ff
74
ff
ff
f
f
f
p
78
tr
pp
p
tr
pp
f
83
tr
ff
87
ff
1.
2.
p

pp
p
pp
f
ff
f
f
f
f
ca – – lan – –
do – – – –
pp
pp

112
117
122
128
133
137

141
147
p
f
152
sf
sf
sf
tr
156
tr
159
ff
p
163

e) as in mm. 45–46

194
rinf.
f
197
f
f
200
sf
sf
sf
sf
203
ff
208
ff
ff
f
f
f
p
pp
213
rinf.
f
pp
ff
tr

218
ffp
222
pp
pp
226
cresc.
229
232
fp
tr
p

Adagio (♪ = 54)

10
13
16
19
sf
22
sf
sf
25
ff

f) As in the first edition; some later editions print G-sharp instead of G.

48
52
ff
p
56
sf
p
pp
59
sf
62
sf
65
sf
p

68
71
p
ff
ff
p
75
p
79
sf
sf
sf
f
sf pp
pp
SCHERZO
Allegro (𝅗𝅥. = 80)
p
p
9
p
f

16/17
24
32
40
49
58
p
f
sf
pp
(p)
ff
1.
2.

TRIO
1.
2.
sf

CODA
Scherzo D.C.
e poi la Coda

Allegro assai (♩. = 116)
p
fp
f
p
sf
sf

32
36
41
45
51
(cresc.)
57

98
dolce
105
p
113
119
sf
125
p
131

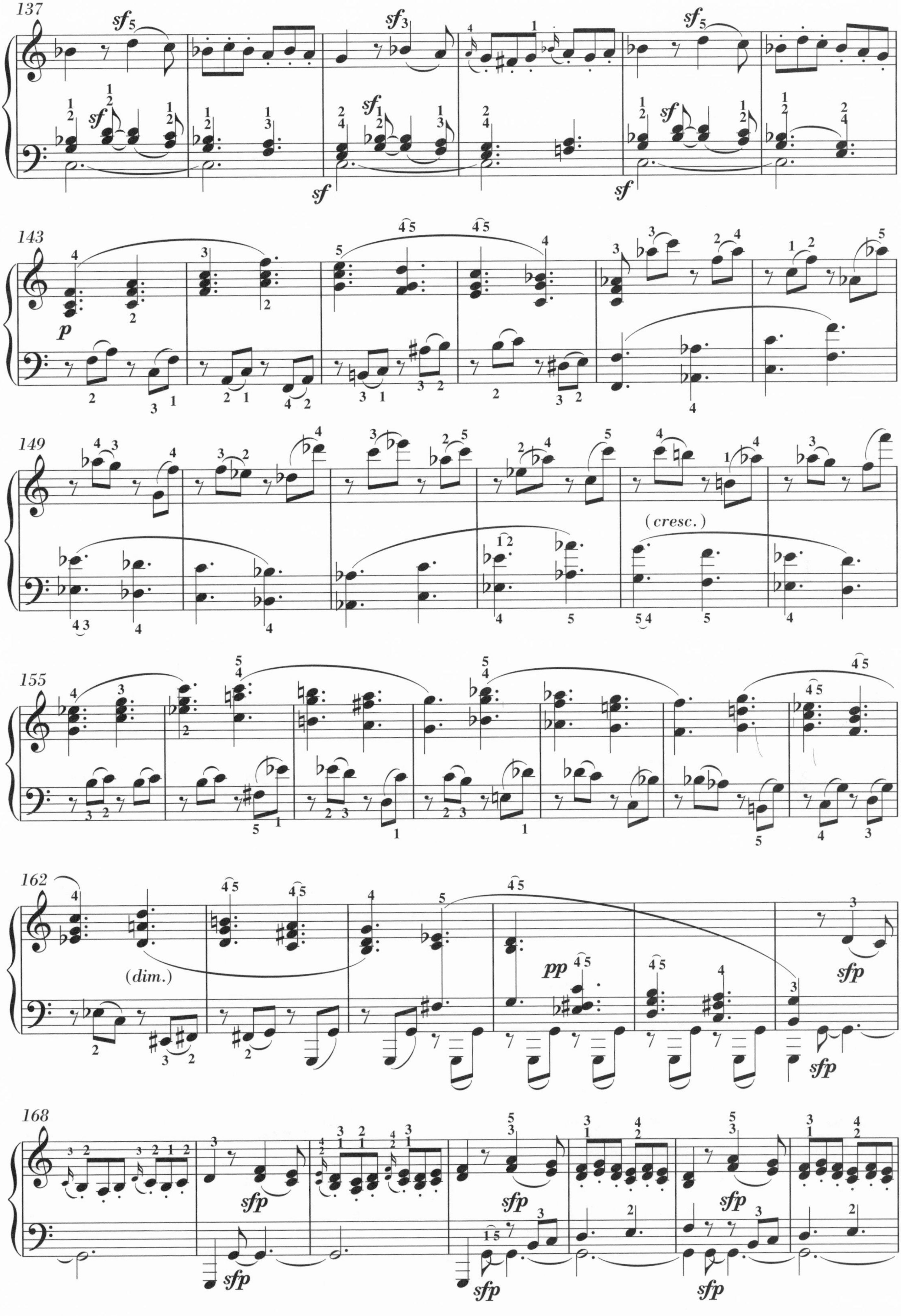
137
143
p
149
(cresc.)
155
162
(dim.)
pp
sfp
168
sfp

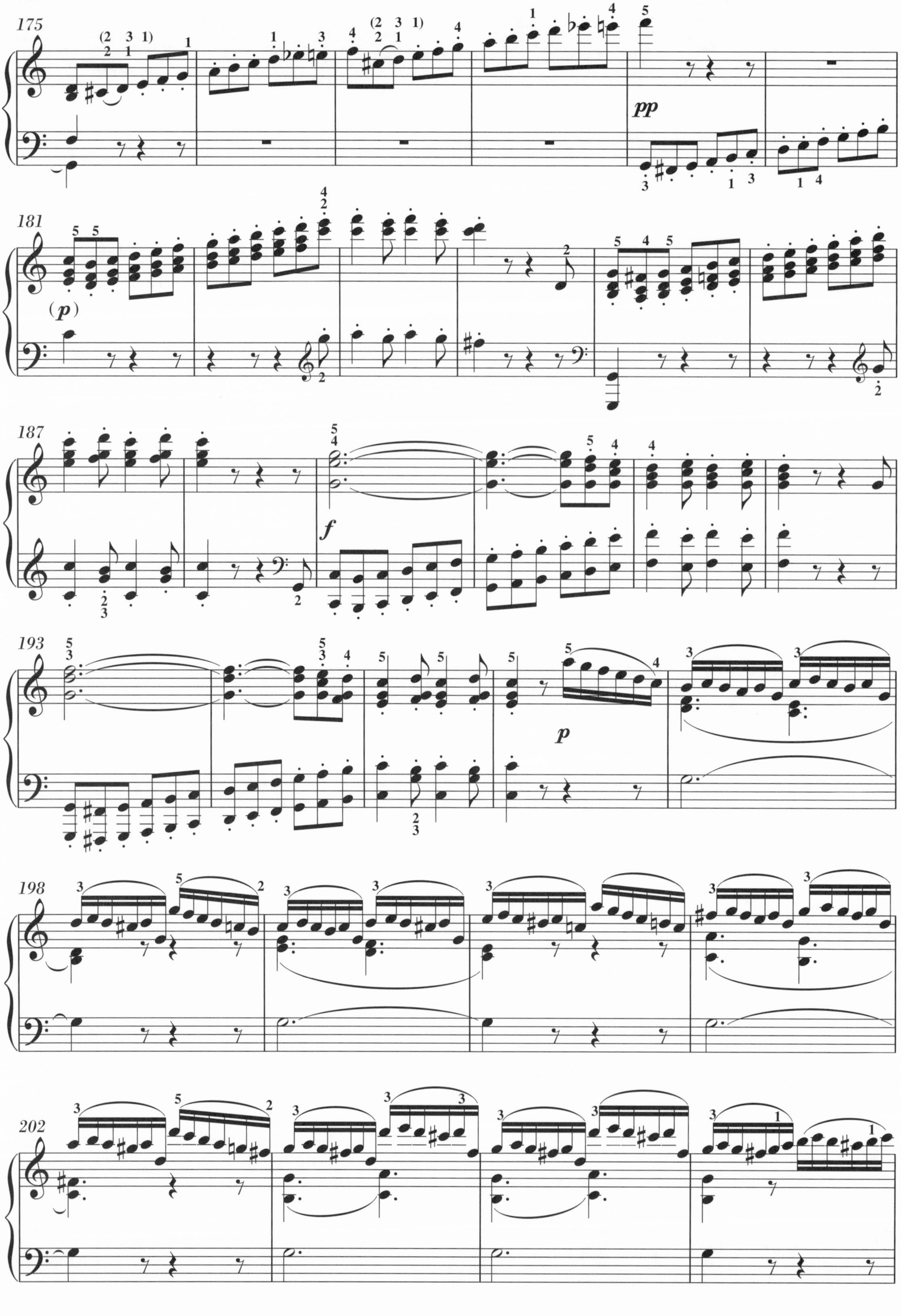

175

pp

181

(*p*)

187

f

193

p

198

206
fp
211
tr
ff
217
p
sf
sf
221
sf
sf
225
p
sf
sf
230
p
sf
sf
p
sf
sf

cresc.
1323

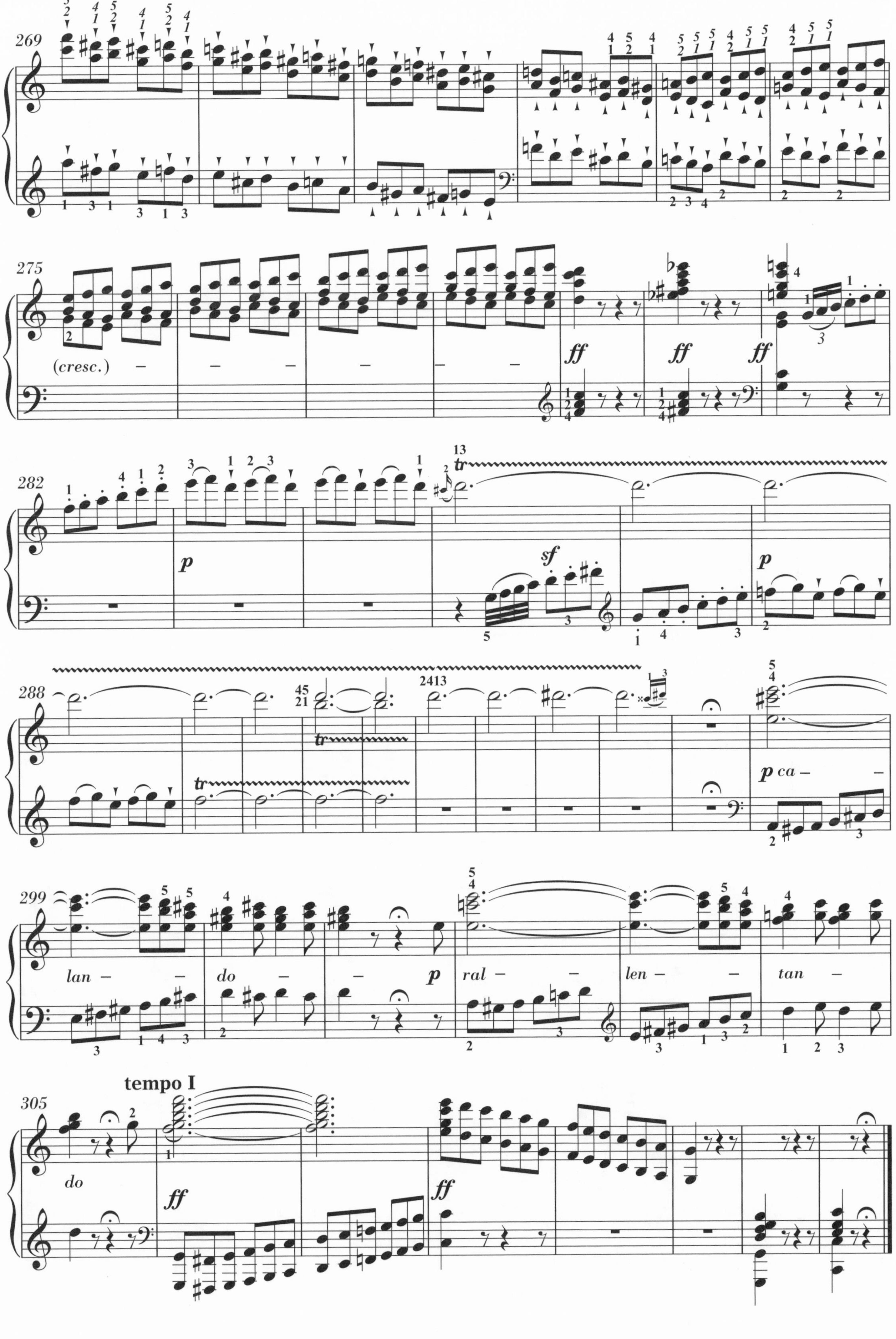

(cresc.)

ca – lan – do – ral – len – tan – do

tempo I

Dedicated to Countess Babette von Keglevics

Sonata in E-flat Major

Opus 7
Composed in 1797

Copyright © 2010 by G. Schirmer, Inc. (ASCAP) New York, NY
International Copyright Secured. All Rights Reserved.

33
sf
sf
fp
40
sf
sf
46
sf
52
sf
58
p
sf
66

a) The accidentals in brackets are lacking in the first edition (Artaria 1797). It is possible that this was an error in the first edition, or an intentional difference from m. 64.

100
ff
sf
sf
104
sf
p
107
ff
111
sf
sf
114
sf
117
sf
sf

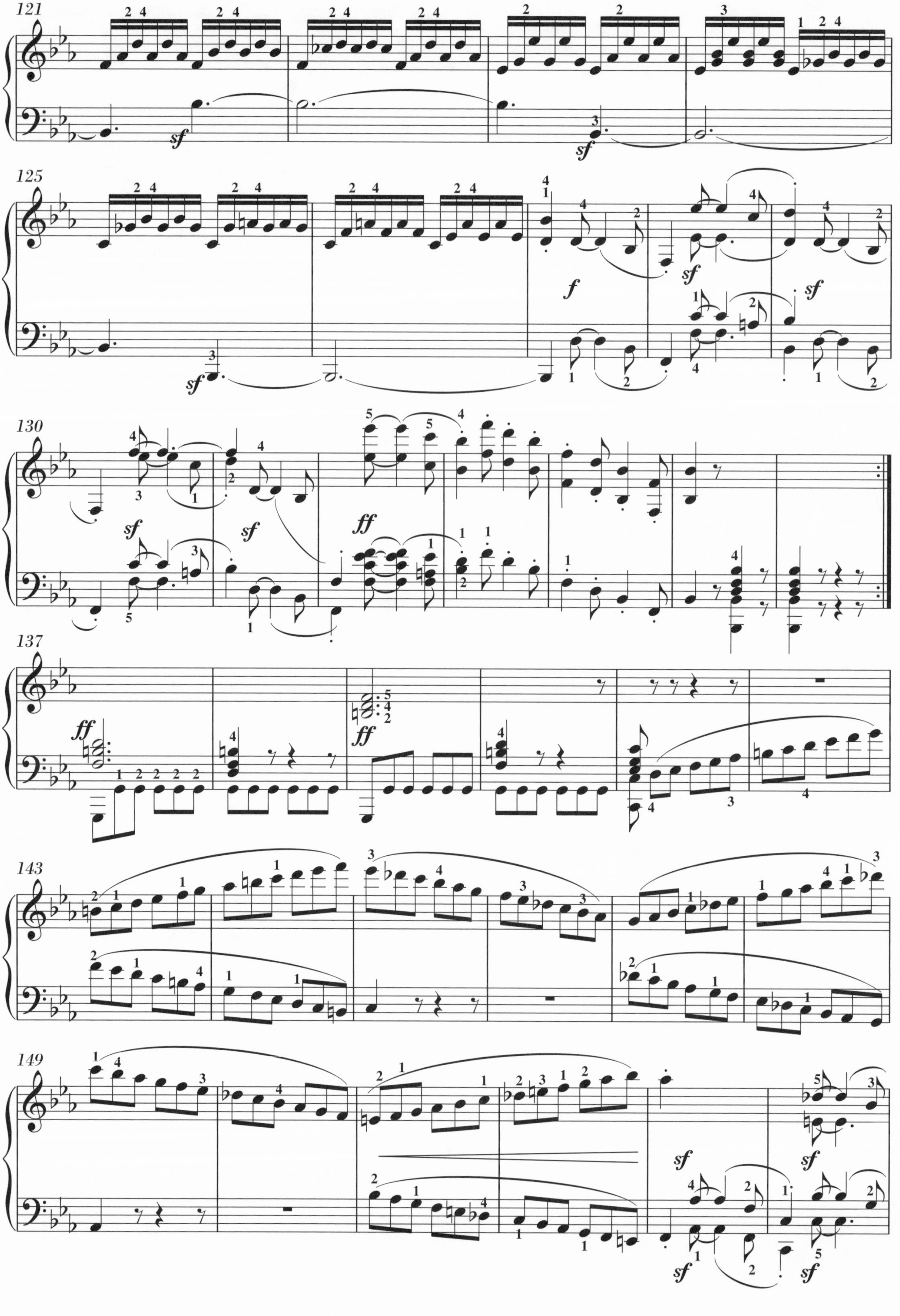
121
sf
sf
125
sf
f
sf
sf
130
sf
sf
ff
137
ff
ff
143
149
sf
sf
sf
sf

155
161
167
decresc.
173
179
185

b) In the first edition, the flat sign before G is missing, however, G-flat is necessary here owing to the harmony of the next phrase.

231
sf
sf
237
p
245
sf
252
cresc.
258
ff
pp
265

271
277
281
285
cresc.
288
292

c) RH under LH

328
cresc.
334
f
ff
sf
340
sf
sf
sf
pp
346
pp
cresc.
353
f
357
ff
ff
ff

Largo, con gran espressione (♪ = 76)
p
sf
sf
p
tenute
rinf.
sfp
fp
f
pp
rinf.
sf
sf
sf
sf
pp
ff
ff
pp
pp
sempre tenuto
sf

29
33
tenuto
staccato
37
ten.
ten.
ten.
45
50
tenuto
57
tenute
rinf.

sfp
f
rinf.
sf
sf
sf
sf
pp
ff
ff
pp
f
f
p
sf
sf
f
f
ff
ff
sf
p
pp
pp
pp
ffp
ffp
pp

Allegro (♩. = 66)
p dolce
pp
sf
man – can – do
pp
dolce

pp
decresc.
cresc.
1.
2.
Fine

95/96
Minore
pp
ffp
100
ffp
104
p
decresc.
108
pp
p
113
ffp
118
ffp

122
f
p
126
ffp
130
ffp
sf
sf
135
ff
139
pp
143
ppp
Allegro D.C.

RONDO

Poco allegretto e grazioso (♩ = 63)

26
f
30
f
fp
pp
34
sf
p
tr
39
f
tr
p
44
f
p
ff
47
sf
p
decresc.
cresc.

51
57
sf
62
p
sf
ff
sf
67
sf
70
1.
2.
71b
ff

74
77
80
83
86
1.
88b
2.
decresc.

91
(a tempo)
ritard.
pp
(p)
95
100
105
rinf.
110
114
rinf.

rinf.
f
fp
pp
p
sf
tr

143
147
fp
sf
sf
151
sf
sf
sf
cresc.
f
f
155
pp
pp
159
pp
ffp
ffp
163
f
p
cresc.

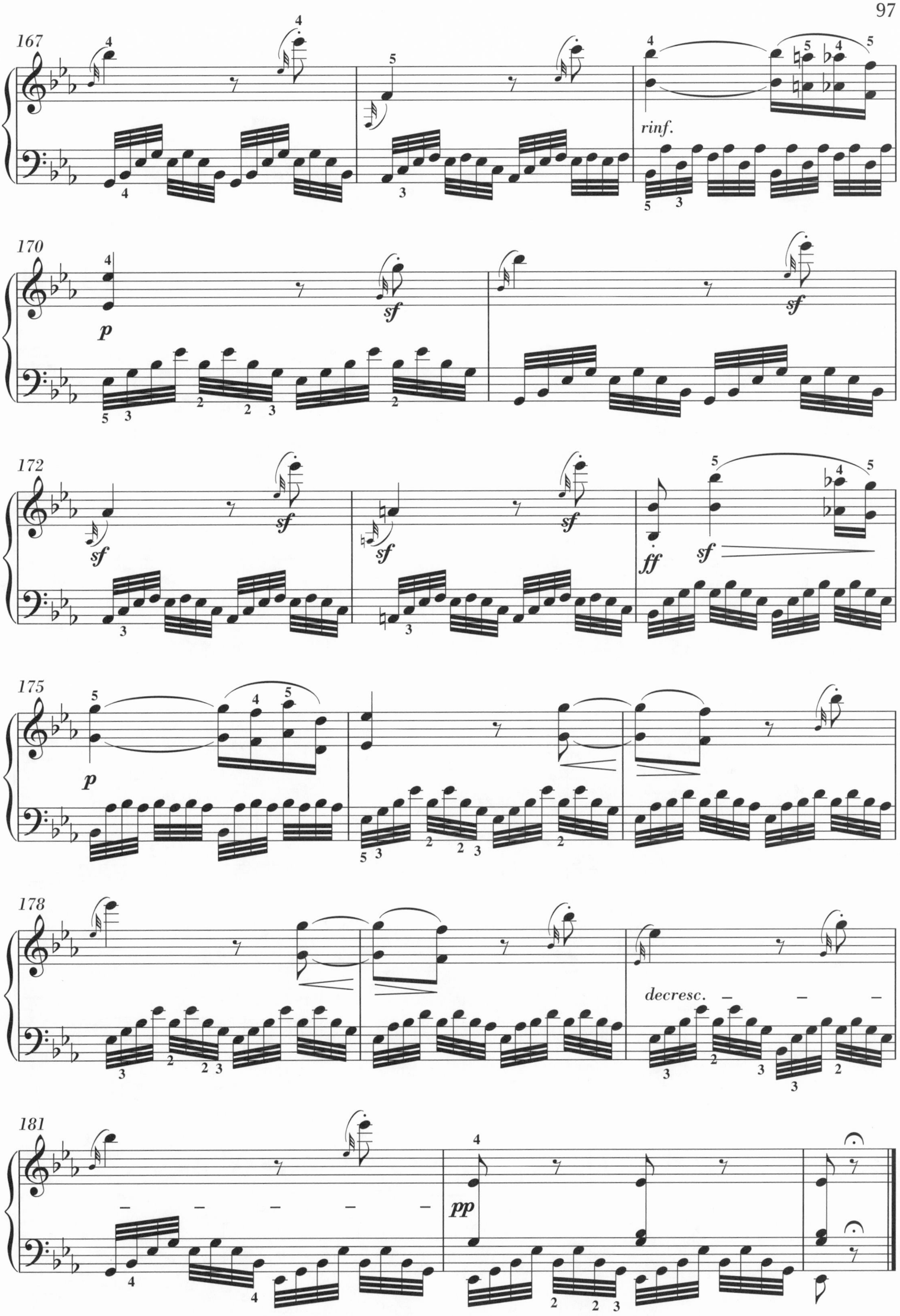
167
rinf.
170
p
sf
sf
172
sf
sf
sf
sf
ff
sf
175
p
178
decresc.
181
pp

Dedicated to Countess von Browne

Sonata in C minor

Opus 10 no. 1
Composed 1796–98

Allegro molto e con brio (𝅗𝅥. = 76)

Copyright © 2010 by G. Schirmer, Inc. (ASCAP) New York, NY
International Copyright Secured. All Rights Reserved.

b)
cresc.
b)

c) As in the first edition.

191
p
fp
201
p
211
218
225
sf
sf
232
f
sf

239
246
cresc.
253
cresc.
260
267
275

g) The arpeggio is played on the fourth sixteenth note.

h) The turn is played before the E-flat so that that note retains its full thirty-second-note value.

j) The A-flat in the manuscript (lost), may have been tied.

i)

ff
p
fp
sfp
pp
cresc.
f
sf

cresc.
rinf.
f
sf
sf
p
rinf.
sf
rinf.
sf
f
p
k)
pp
de – – cre – – scen – – do
pp
k)

FINALE
Prestissimo (𝅗𝅥 = 96)

30
(cresc.)
ff
34
ff
ff
38
p
ff
ff
p
44
sf
p
sf
p
sf
p
sf
50
cresc.
ff
55
sf
sf
p

cresc.
ff p
ffp
fp
fp
cresc.
sf
ff

90
ff
94
ff
p
ff
ff
p
100
cresc.
fp
106
ritard.
calando
pp
p
tenuto
113
adagio Tempo I
ff
p
118
de
cres
cen
do

Dedicated to Countess von Browne

Sonata in F Major

Opus 10 no. 2
Composed in 1796–98

Copyright © 2010 by G. Schirmer, Inc. (ASCAP) New York, NY
International Copyright Secured. All Rights Reserved.

ff
sf
sf
f
pp
cresc.
f
sf
f
p
f
tr
p
f
tr
ff
cresc.
ff
ff
1.
2.

67
p
72
c)
f
77
fp
81
cresc.
fp
85
cresc.
89
ff
fp
c)

cresc.
p
cresc.
f
cresc.
f
ff
sf
sf
decresc.
p
pp

117/118
p
125
pp
131
pp
136/137
p
143
cresc.
sf
148
cresc.
sf

p
ff
sf
f

pp
cresc.
f
sf
f
ff
p
f
tr
p
f
tr
ff
tr
sf
cresc.
tr
ff
ff
1.
2.

d) e) ***p*** as in the first edition (Eder, 1798) f)

59

67

75

83

cresc.

92

100

cresc.

108

119
pp
p
128
cresc.
136
sf
143
sf
tr
pp
149
rinf.
156
rinf.
164
fp
tr
cresc.
f

Presto (♩ = 160)
sf
f
fp

sf
fp
f
sf
sf
sf
sf
sf
sf
sf
sf
sf
sf
sf
sf
sf
sf
sf
sf
sf
f
p

69
p
77
cresc.
85
f
ff
91
97
103
p

cresc.
f
ff
sf
f
sf
sf
f
fp
cresc.
ff

Dedicated to Countess von Browne

Sonata in D Major

Opus 10 no. 3
Composed in 1796–98

a) Beethoven's own fingerings in italics. b) The lowest note of Beethoven's piano at this time was FF. c) The first edition (Eder 1798) has no octaves here. d) The highest note of Beethoven's piano at this time was f³.

Copyright © 2010 by G. Schirmer, Inc. (ASCAP) New York, NY
International Copyright Secured. All Rights Reserved.

e) short appoggiatura

60
p
66
sf
sf
p
pp
cresc.
73
sf
sf
sf
p
79
sf
sf
sf
p
sf
sf
85
p
cresc.
sf
sf
sf
sf
ff
92
fp

f) No tie in LH in the first edition; the same, m. 285.

138
ff
143
sf
sf
sf
148
ff
ff
153
sf
sf
sf
ff
ff
158
163
ff

g) In the first edition the next four LH pitches are *f*, but the chord in m. 183 is *sf*.

203
209
214
219
224
229
cresc.
cresc.

h) As in the first edition (Eder) and in the Gesamtausgabe.

270
sf
sf
ff
fp
276
fp
281
cresc.
sf
ff
286
pp
294
cresc.
f
pp
sf
pp
303
pp
pp

310
317
sf
323
sf
cresc.
p
329
334
cresc.
339
ff

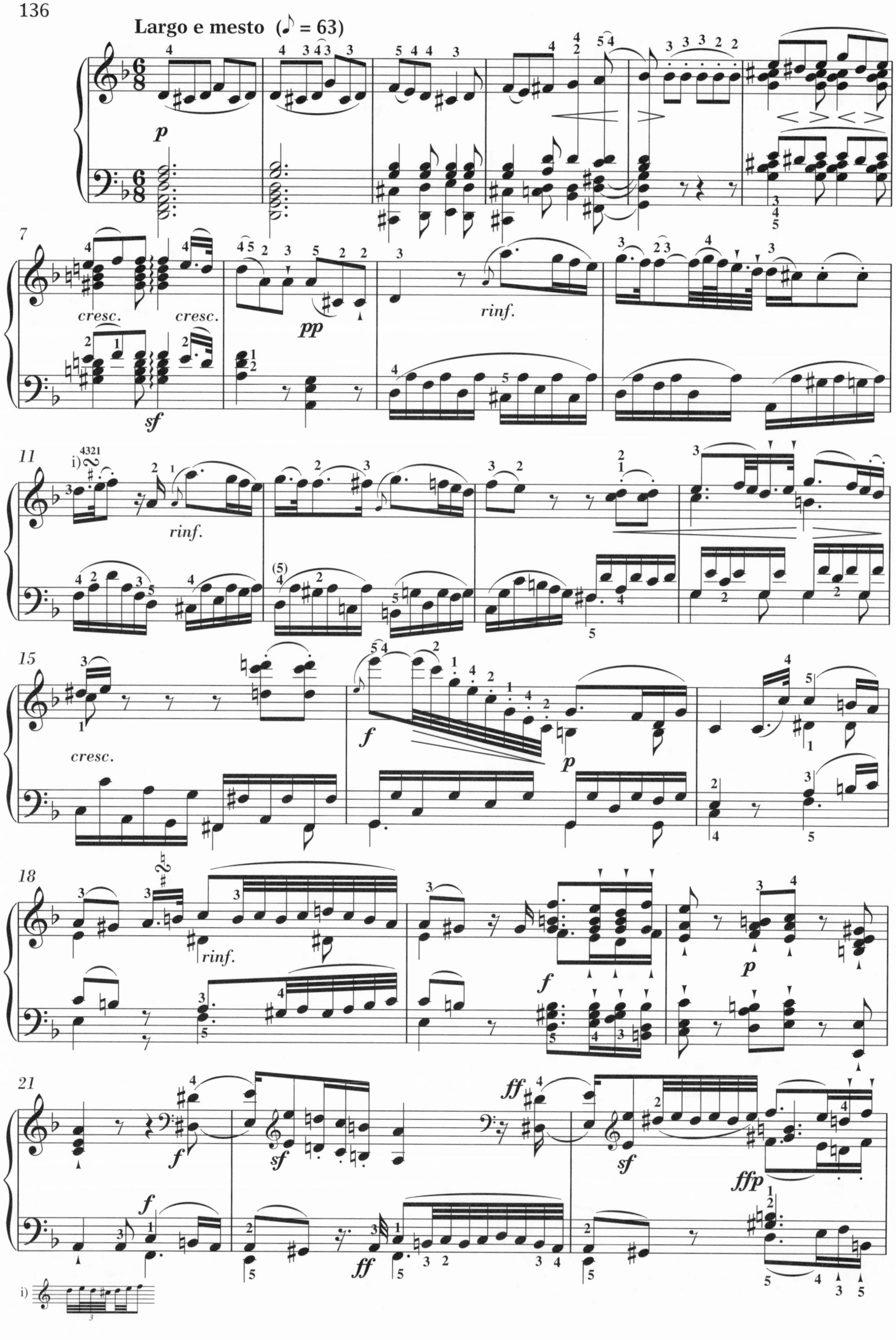

Largo e mesto (♪ = 63)

ffp
ffp
pp
cresc.
cresc.
ff
sf
p
p
p
p
rinf.
cresc.
ff
ff
ff
ff
f
p
fp
f
p
fp
fp

40
fp
smorzando
42
pp
f
sf
decresc.
45
rinf.
rinf.
rinf.
decresc.
pp
50
cresc.
fp
54
cresc.
f
p
p
57
(rinf.)
f
p
f

61
sf
ff
ff
sf
ffp
ffp
ffp
64
p
pp
6
66
cresc.
67
f
f
68
sf
sf
69
sf
sf

ff
f
p
fp
pp
cresc.
f
rinf.
dim.
rinf.
pp

j) This slur appears in the first edition.

54/55 TRIO
60
65
71
76
81
Men. D.C. ma senza replica

RONDO

Allegro (♩ = 144)

k) short appoggiatura

cresc.
sf
sf
sf
p
cresc.
ff
sf
p
cresc.
f
p
pp
cresc.
p
ff
p
ff
sf
sf

decresc.
cresc.

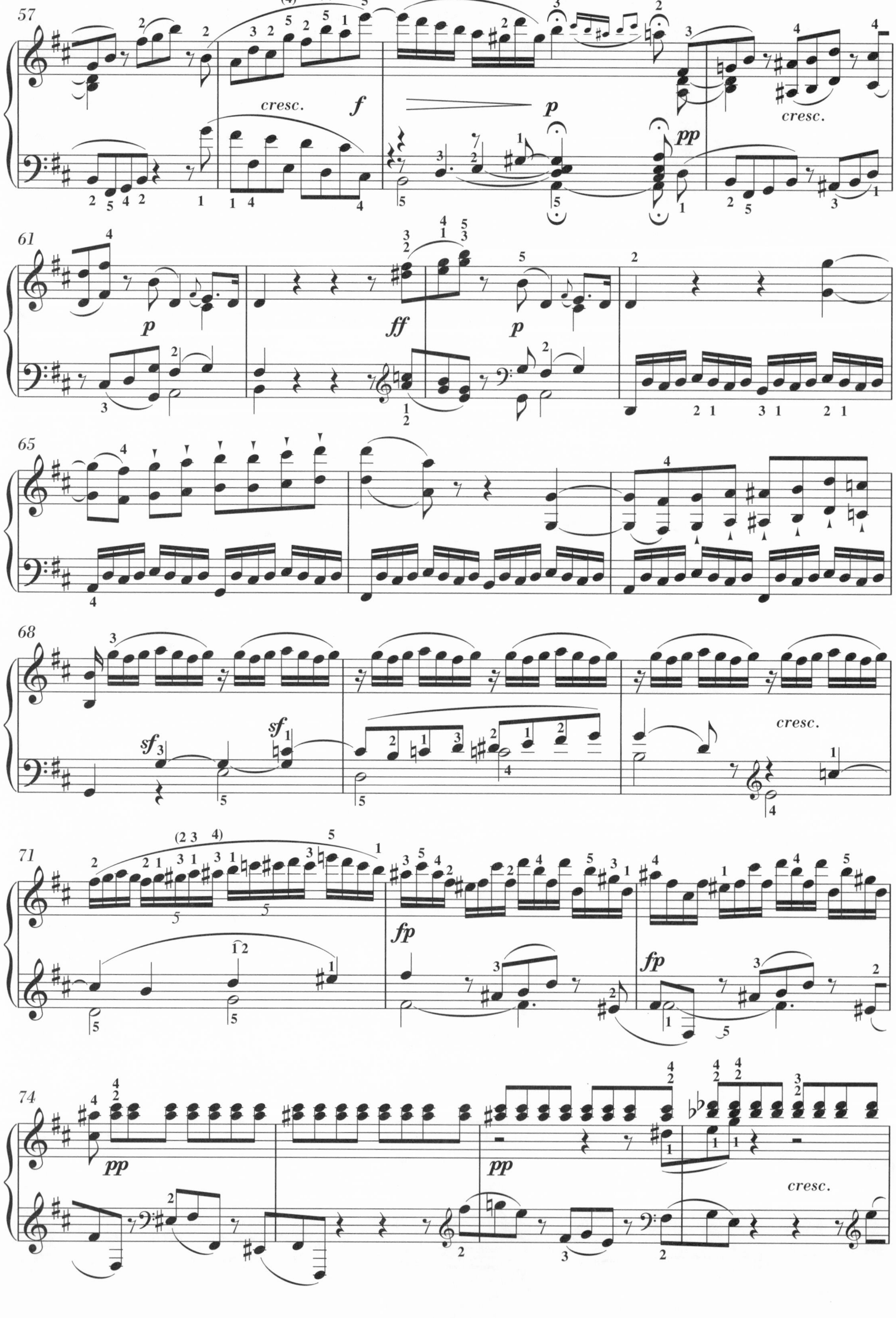

57

cresc. ***f*** ***p*** ***pp*** *cresc.*

61

p ***ff*** ***p***

65

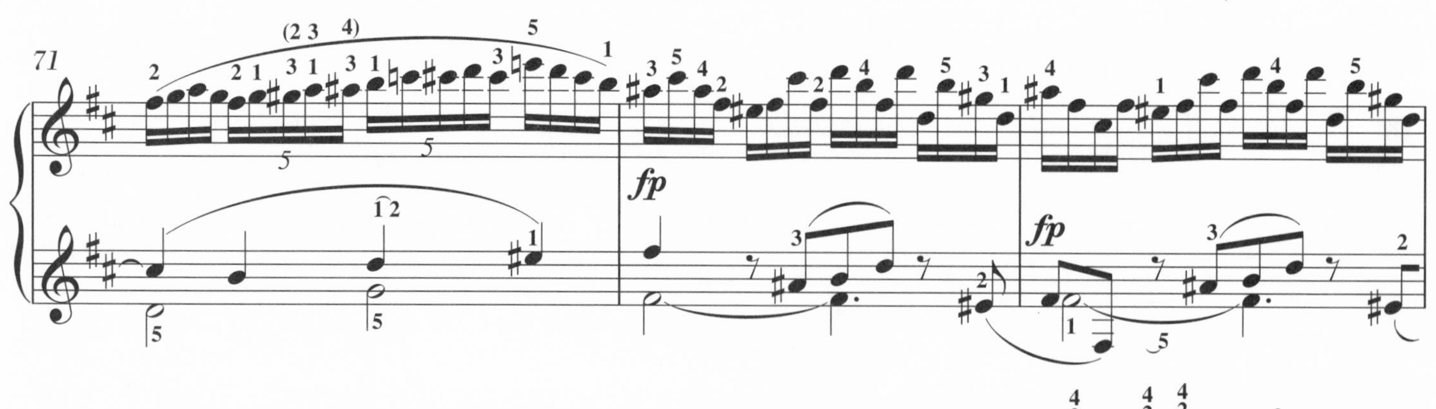

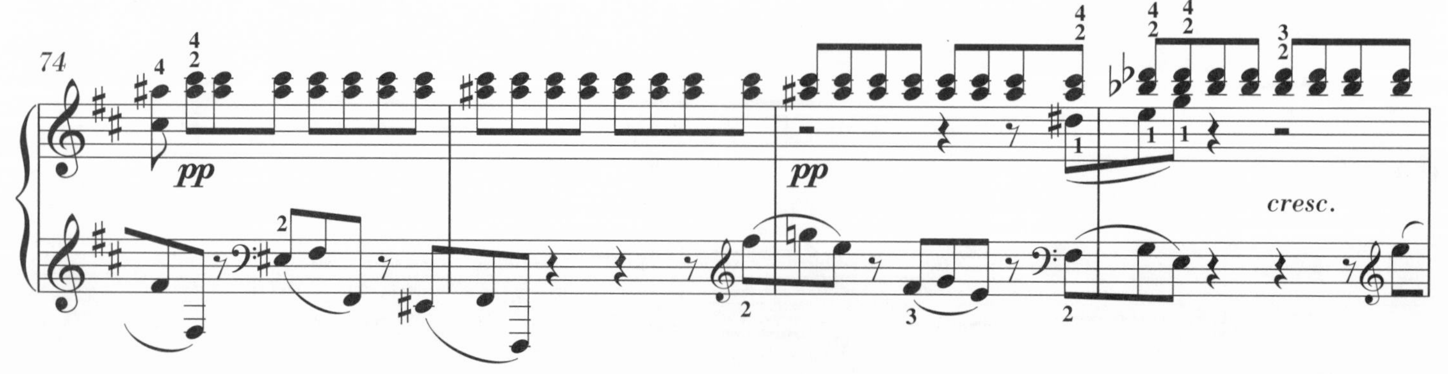

sf
sf
sf
sf
p
cresc.
sf
pp
cresc.
f
p
pp
cresc.
p
ff
sf
sf
sf
sf
sf
sf
sf
sf
sf
sf
sf

98
p
pp
pp
101
pp
104
fp
107
109
111

Dedicated to Prince Carl von Lichnowsky

Sonata in C minor
(Pathétique)

Opus 13
Composed in 1798–99

a) three triplets b) two triplets c) play evenly; no sub-division

Copyright © 2010 by G. Schirmer, Inc. (ASCAP) New York, NY
International Copyright Secured. All Rights Reserved.

d) as in the first edition; subsequent editions have [music example] e) LH over RH f) short appoggiatura

g) as in the first edition; subsequent editions have

101
p
cresc.
106
111
f
p
116
cresc.
120
f
126
1.
2.
ff

Tempo I

133

fp *fp* *fp* *p* *decresc.* *pp*

Allegro molto e con brio

137

p *cresc.* *f* *p* *cresc.*

144

f *p* *cresc.*

150

156

162

p

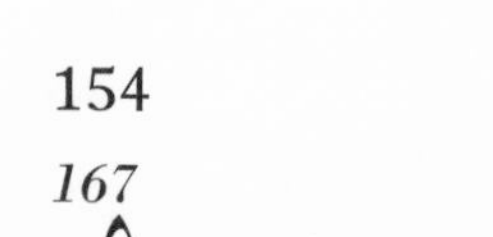

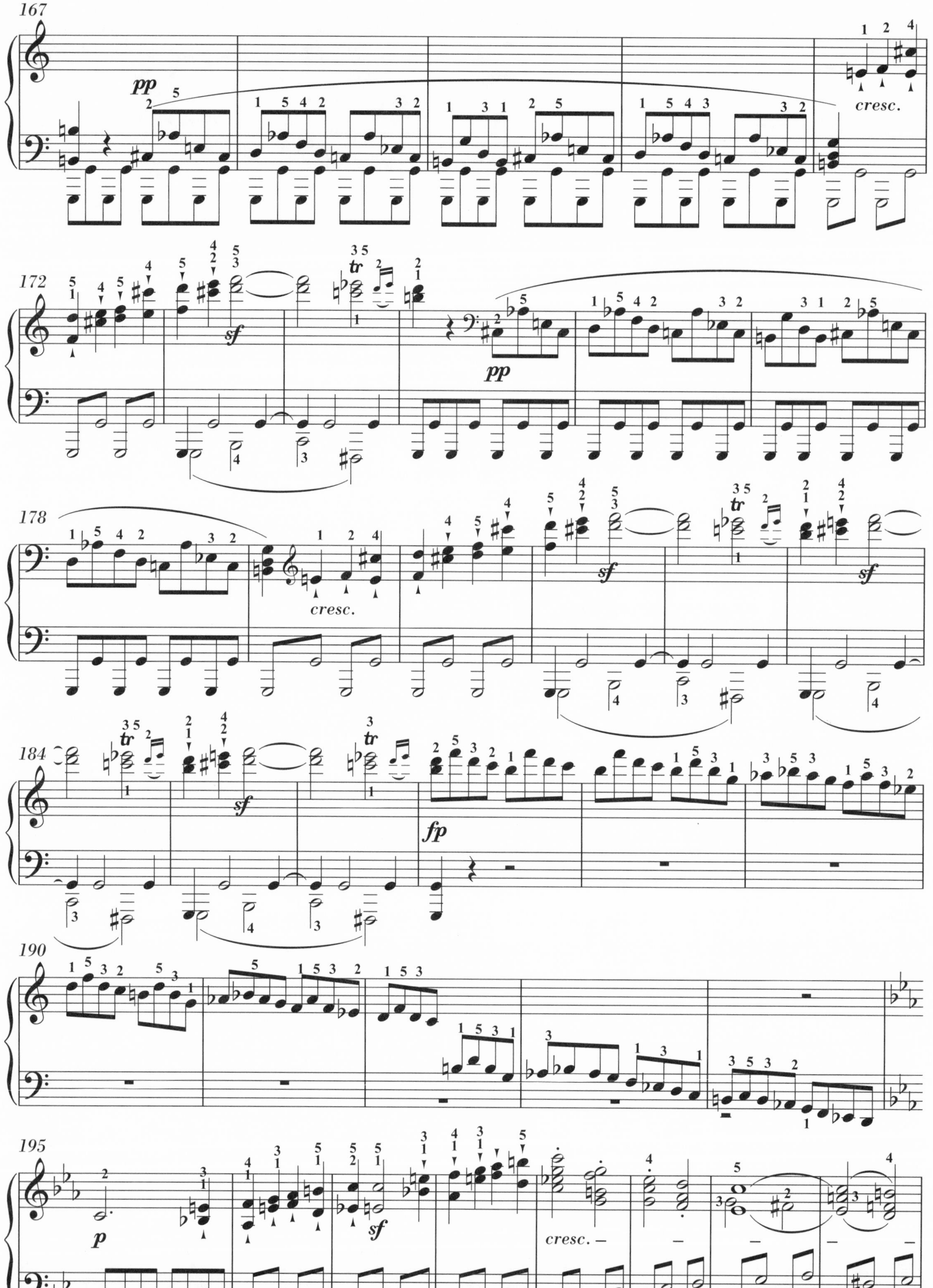
167
pp
cresc.
172
sf
tr
pp
178
cresc.
sf
tr
sf
184
tr
sf
tr
fp
190
195
p
sf
cresc. –

203
p
sf
cresc.
211
p
cresc.
p
cresc.
p
220
sf
sf
228
sf
sf
236
sf
sf
244
decresc.
pp

253
p
257
cresc.
261
f
265
p
269
cresc.
273
f

Grave
Allegro molto e con brio
cresc.
decresc.

h) 3⁀4 first, then 1⁀2 i)

pp
p
pp
cresc.
sf
sf
sf
fp
decresc.
pp

48
cresc.
51
p
55
58
61
64
pp

j) [music example] k) short appoggiatura

dolce
cresc.
p
sf
sf
cresc.
(p)
p
sf
cresc.
p

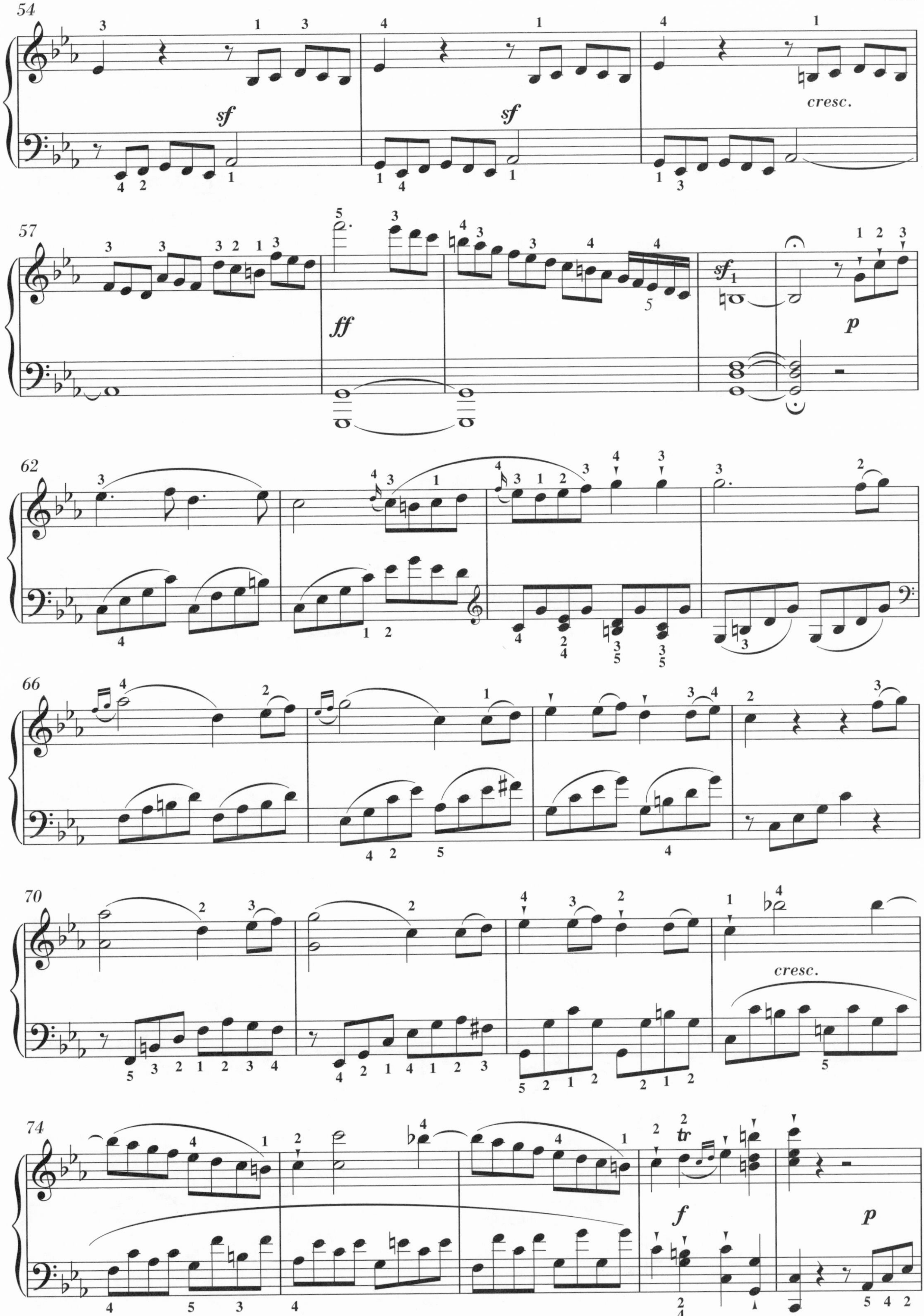
54
sf
sf
cresc.
57
ff
sf
p
62
66
70
cresc.
74
tr
f
p

79
p
89
98
cresc.
103
f
sf
cresc.
108
ff
112
sf
sf
sf

116 *ff* *sf* *p*

122

127

132 *sf* *p* *dolce*

137 *cresc.*

143 (*p*)

147
151
p
157
165
calando
p
172
177
cresc.

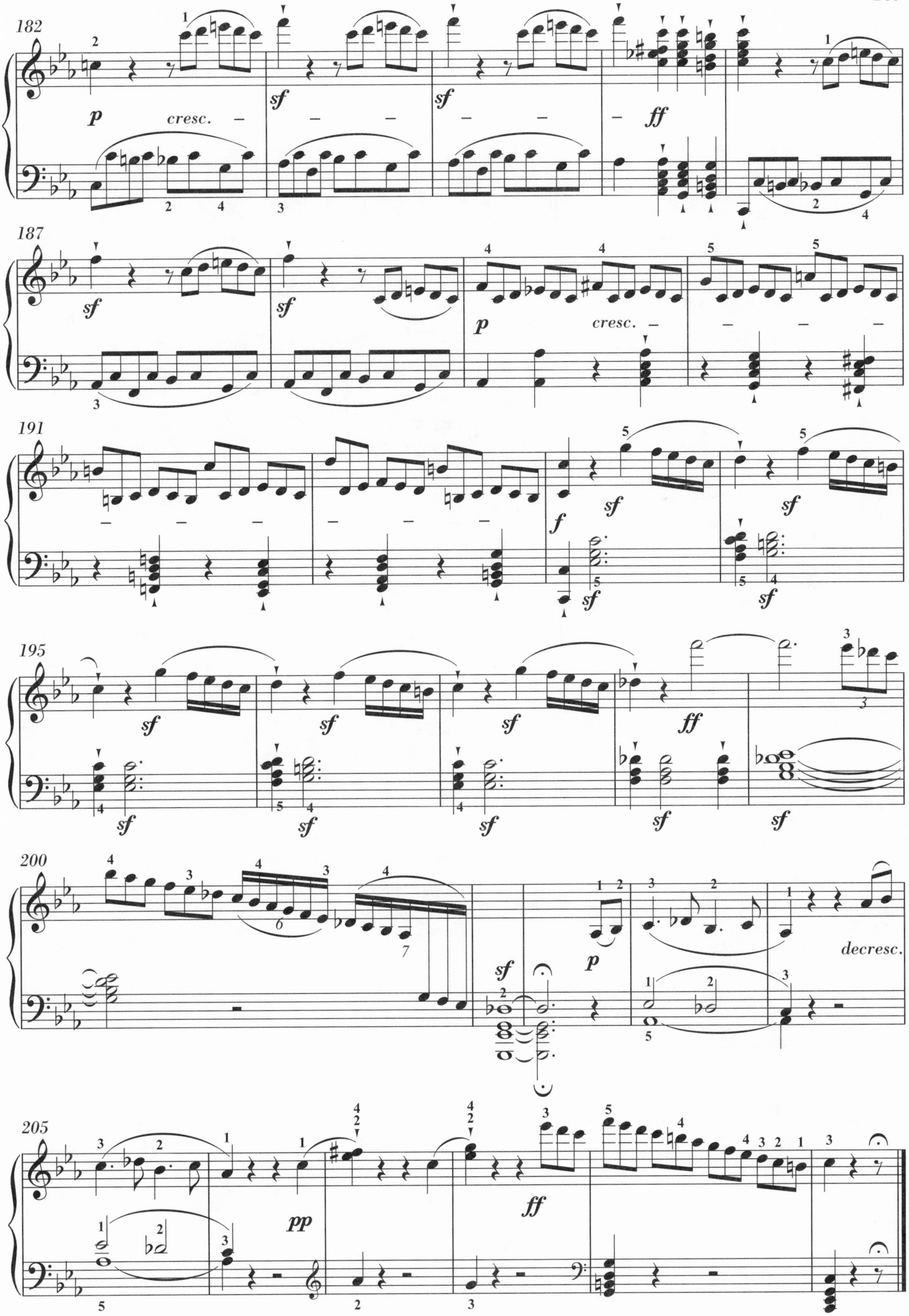
182
p
cresc.
sf
sf
ff
187
sf
sf
p
cresc.
191
f
sf
sf
195
sf
sf
sf
ff
sf
200
sf
p
decresc.
205
pp
ff

Copyright © 2010 by G. Schirmer, Inc. (ASCAP) New York, NY
International Copyright Secured. All Rights Reserved.

32
38
a)
43
48
53
59
cresc.
1.
2.
a)

63
cresc.
(fp)
66
69
cresc.
p
cresc.
72
rinf.
75
p
pp
78
cresc.
sf

p
decresc.
f
sf
p
decresc.

103
pp
cresc.
106
f
f
p
f
110
p
sf
f
p
115
121
p
p
127
p

b) Thus in the first editions of Mollo and Simrock; in some recent editions, this passage is changed in accordance with mm. 44–45, a version which could not be played on Beethoven's pianos with their more limited registral range.

Allegretto (♩. = 50)
p
sf
cresc.
sf
sf
p
sf
sf
p
p
sf
p
cresc.
sf
sf
sf
cresc.
p
cresc.

54
f
sf
sf
p
pp
cresc.
sf
sf
63 Maggiore
p
73
p
p
82
p cresc.
decresc.
p
92
decresc.
pp
Allegretto da capo
e poi la Coda
CODA
101
p
p decresc.
pp

RONDO
Allegro comodo (𝅗𝅥 = 80)
p
cresc.
(f)
p
sf
pp
tr

29
decresc.
pp
p
33
cresc.
(f)
p
sf
38
cresc.
42
sf
46
f
50

p
f
p
decresc.

c) Thus in the first edition, in contrast to m. 25. The dominant harmony in m. 25 carries more weight.

104
pp
p
cresc.
110
ff
115
sf
sf
119
sf
decresc.
p
pp
123
p
127
cresc.
tr
f

Dedicated to Baroness Josefa von Braun

Sonata in G Major

Opus 14 no. 2
Composed in 1798–99

a) short appoggiatura b) Play the ornament before beat one, i.e., at the end of the previous measure.

Copyright © 2010 by G. Schirmer, Inc. (ASCAP) New York, NY
International Copyright Secured. All Rights Reserved.

c) Thus in the first editions of Mollo and Simrock; in some recent editions, this passage is changed to be parallel to m. 170. Such a synthetic version would go beyond the highest register of Beethoven's piano.

63
p
pp
68
cresc.
72
f
p
76
decresc.
80
pp
f
84

d) Thus in the first editions; in some recent editions as in m. 4: compare footnote to m. 43 with regard to register.

decresc.
pp
(cresc.)
f
ff
sf
p
cresc.
tr

139
cresc.
p
cresc.
144
p
149
153
p
159
164
cresc. –
p

169 *cresc.* **f** **sf** **f**

173 **sf** **p** *dolce* **p**

179 *cresc.*

184 *decresc.* *cresc.*

189 *rinf.* **p** *cresc.* **f** **sf**

195 **p** **p**

Andante (𝅗𝅥 = 72)
La prima parte senza replica
p
cresc.
sf
cresc.
sf
p
p
cresc.
p
f
sf
p
sf
sf
sf
sf
sf
sf
sf
sf
p
p
sempre legato

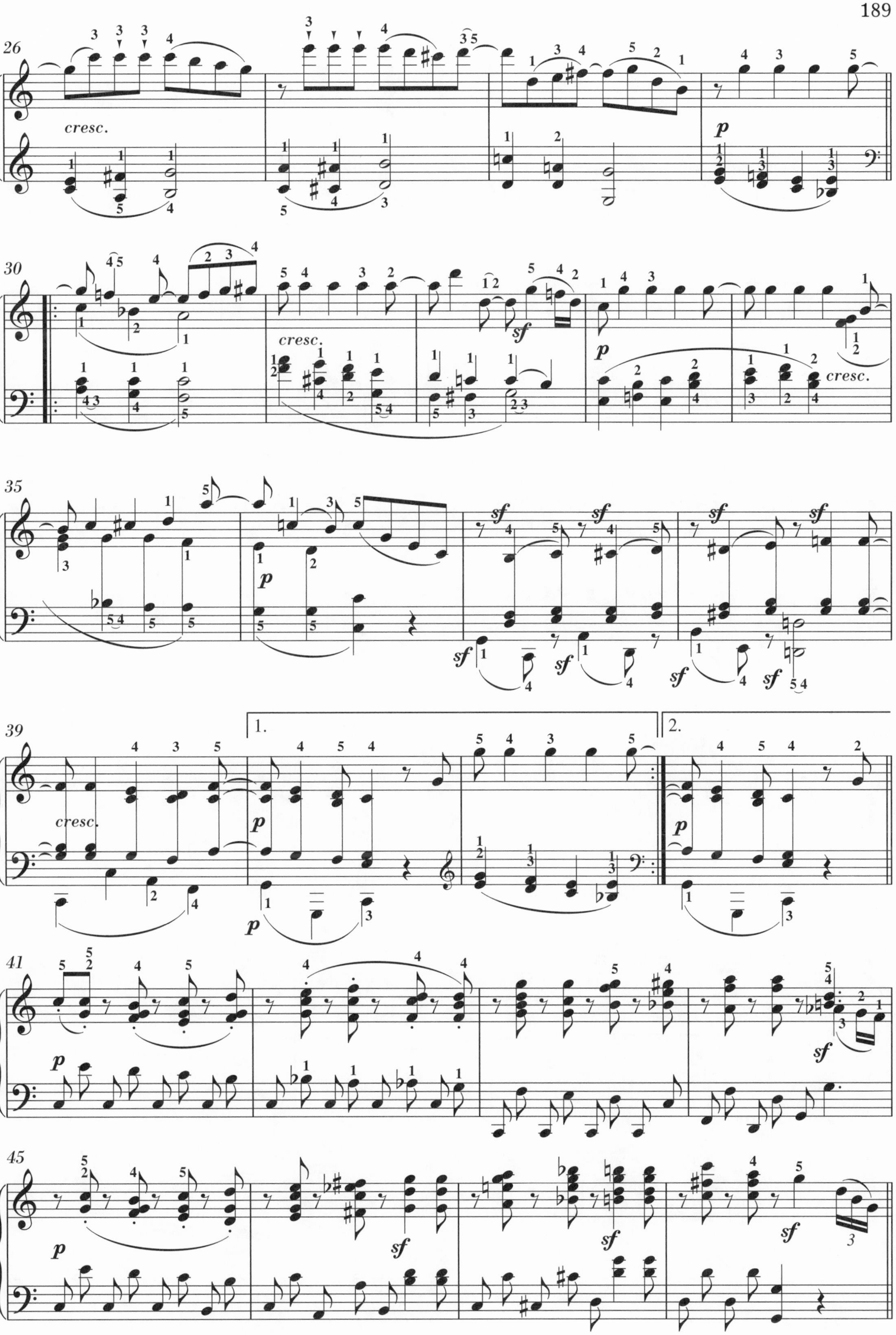
26
cresc.
p
30
cresc.
cresc.
sf
p
35
p
sf
39
1.
2.
cresc.
p
41
p
sf
45
p
sf
3

49
cresc.
53
cresc.
57
cresc.
decresc.
1.
2.
61
decresc.
65
sempre legato
68
cresc.
rinf.

cresc.
rinf.
p
p
p
p
cresc.
p
cresc.
(cresc.)
sf
sf
sf
sf
f
decresc.
p
p
pp
pp
ff

SCHERZO

Allegro assai (♩. = 72)

e) short appoggiatura

49 *sf* *p* *cresc.*

56 *sf* *p*

64 *sf* *sf*

71 *decresc.* *dolce* *p*

78

85 *sf* *sf* *sf* *sf* *sf* *sf*

92
99
105
decresc.
pp
p
112
119
sf
sf
p
126
sf
decresc.

p
p
sf
p
cresc.
f
sf p
f
sf
sf
cresc.
decresc.
pp

181
pp
cresc.
p
187
cresc.
193
sf
sf
sf
199
sf
sf
p
cresc.
205
ff
p
211
cresc.

217 *sf* *sf* *sf*

223 *sf* *sf* *p* *cresc.*

229 *ff* *p*

236 *sf*

242 *sf* *sf* *sf*

248 *p* *pp*

LABORUM
DULCE
LENIMEN
G. SCHIRMER

Dedicated to Countess von Browne

Sonata in B-flat Major

Opus 22
Composed in 1800

Copyright © 2010 by G. Schirmer, Inc. (ASCAP) New York, NY
International Copyright Secured. All Rights Reserved.

a) Many editions print this chord as D–F (see m. 174); however, both the first edition (Hoffmeister & Kühnel, Leipzig) and the copy revised by Beethoven show a G instead of F.

46
sf
f
49
f
f
f
f
52
p
cresc.
ff
sf
55
p
59
decresc.
pp
ff
sf
sf
64
sf
sf
sf
p
ff

b) C also in the revised copy, not B-flat as in some editions.

95

98

101

104

decresc.

p

107

pp

110

113

pp

116

pp

119

cresc.

122

decresc.

125

pp *p*

cresc.

130

fp

cresc.
f
p
sf

c) correct here as G–B-flat; see footnote to m. 43

177
fz
f
180
f
f
f
f
183
p
cresc.
ff
sf
186
p
190
decresc.
pp
ff
sf
sf
195
sf
sf
sf
p
ff

d) short appoggiatura e) The turn can be played on the second sixteenth of the second eighth. f) Play the turn before the sixteenth-note B-flat.

21
24
cresc.
sf
p
26
cresc.
sf
27
p
sf
p
cresc.
30
p
pp
pp
pp
33
pp
cresc.
sf
sf
36
sf
sf
sf
cresc.

39
p
41
43
cresc.
p
cresc.
p
cresc.
p
45
p
cresc.
pp
47
50
cresc.
p
52
cresc.
(dim.)
tr

cresc.
sf
decresc.
pp
sf
decresc.
pp
p
cresc.
sf
p
cresc.
sf
p
sf
p
sf
cresc.
pp

MENUETTO (♩ = 108)

cresc.
Fine
Minore
Menuetto da capo senza replica

RONDO

Allegretto (♪ = 126)

g) h) Play the turn before the dotted-sixteenth-note C.

i) This bar is configured differently from m. 33 because the range of Beethoven's piano at this time did not extend above f^3. j) without tail

50
cresc.
56
p
61
cresc.
f
p
cresc.
66
p
f
sf
f
f
f
sf
72
p
75
cresc.

78
f
sf
83
89
95
p
98
cresc.
101
fp

105
pp
110
cresc.
p
114
cresc.
118
f
p
p
121
cresc.
124
f

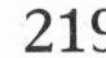

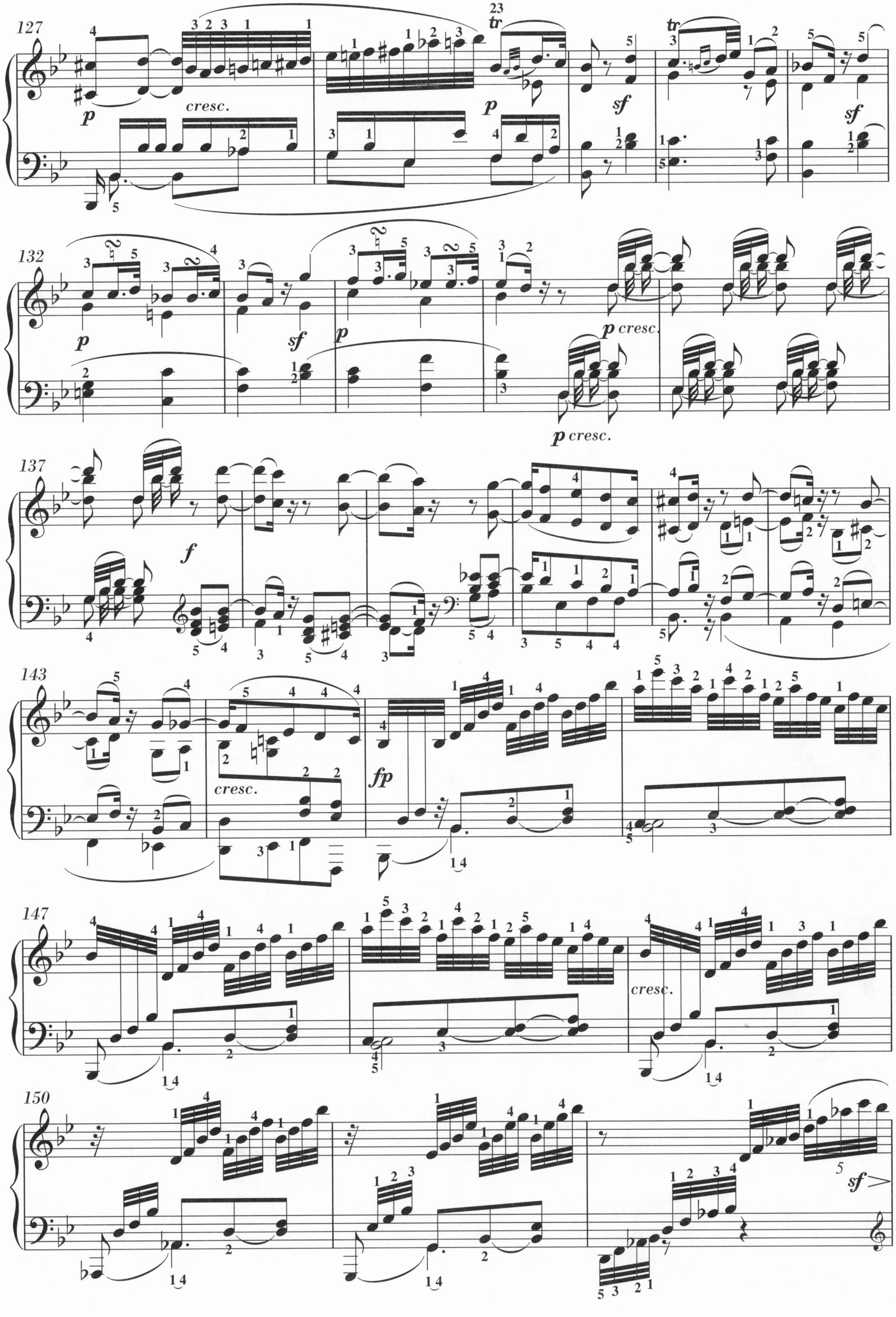
cresc.
p cresc.
p cresc.
cresc.
cresc.

153
p
158
pp
p
163
cresc.
sf
p
166
cresc.
170
p
cresc.
f
p
173
cresc.

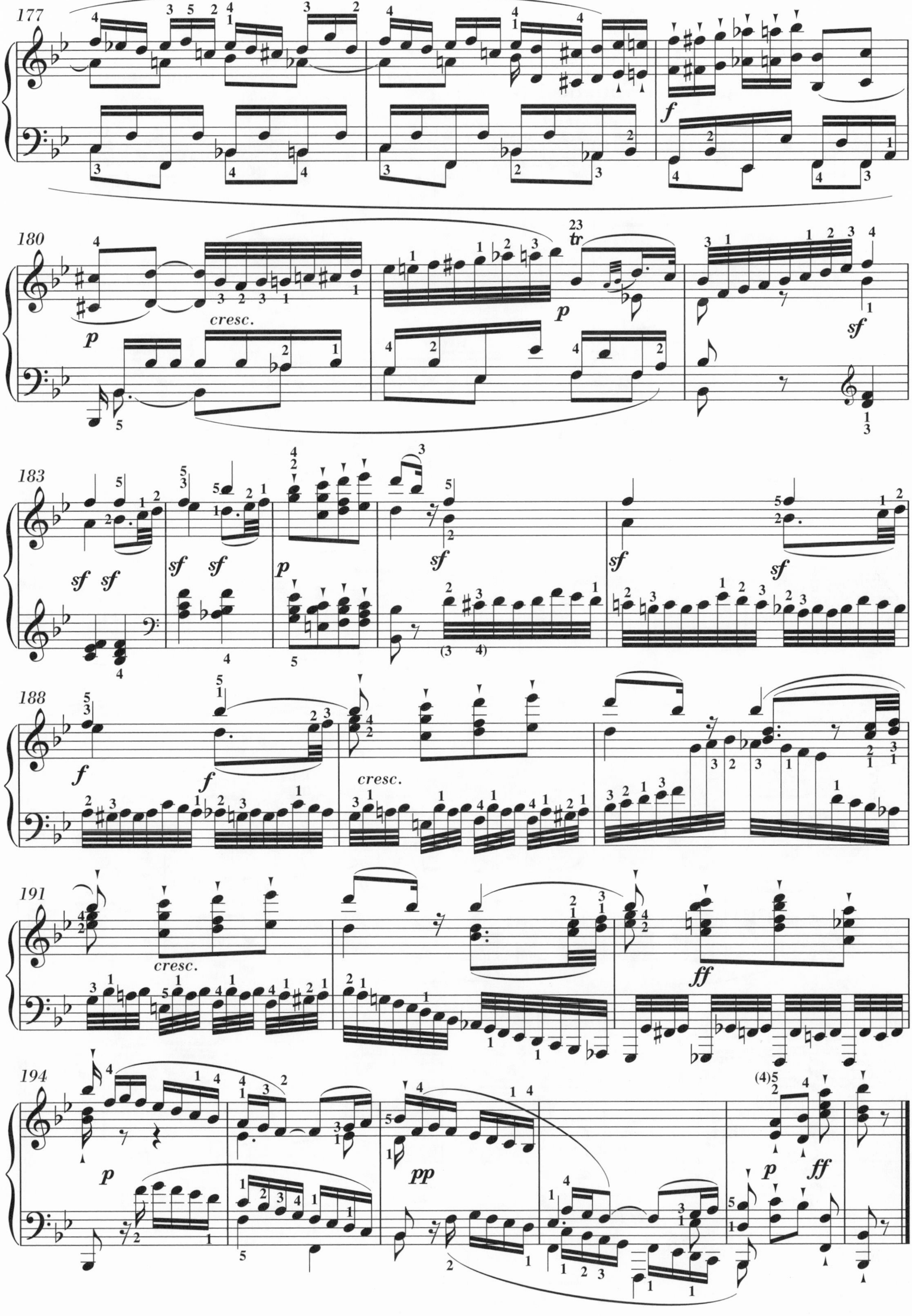
177
180
cresc.
183
188
cresc.
191
cresc.
194

Dedicated to Prince Carl von Lichnowsky

Sonata in A-flat Major

Opus 26
Composed in 1800–01

a) The pedal markings are Beethoven's. b) short appoggiatura

Copyright © 2010 by G. Schirmer, Inc. (ASCAP) New York, NY
International Copyright Secured. All Rights Reserved.

c) Played as in m. 25 of the theme.

Var. II

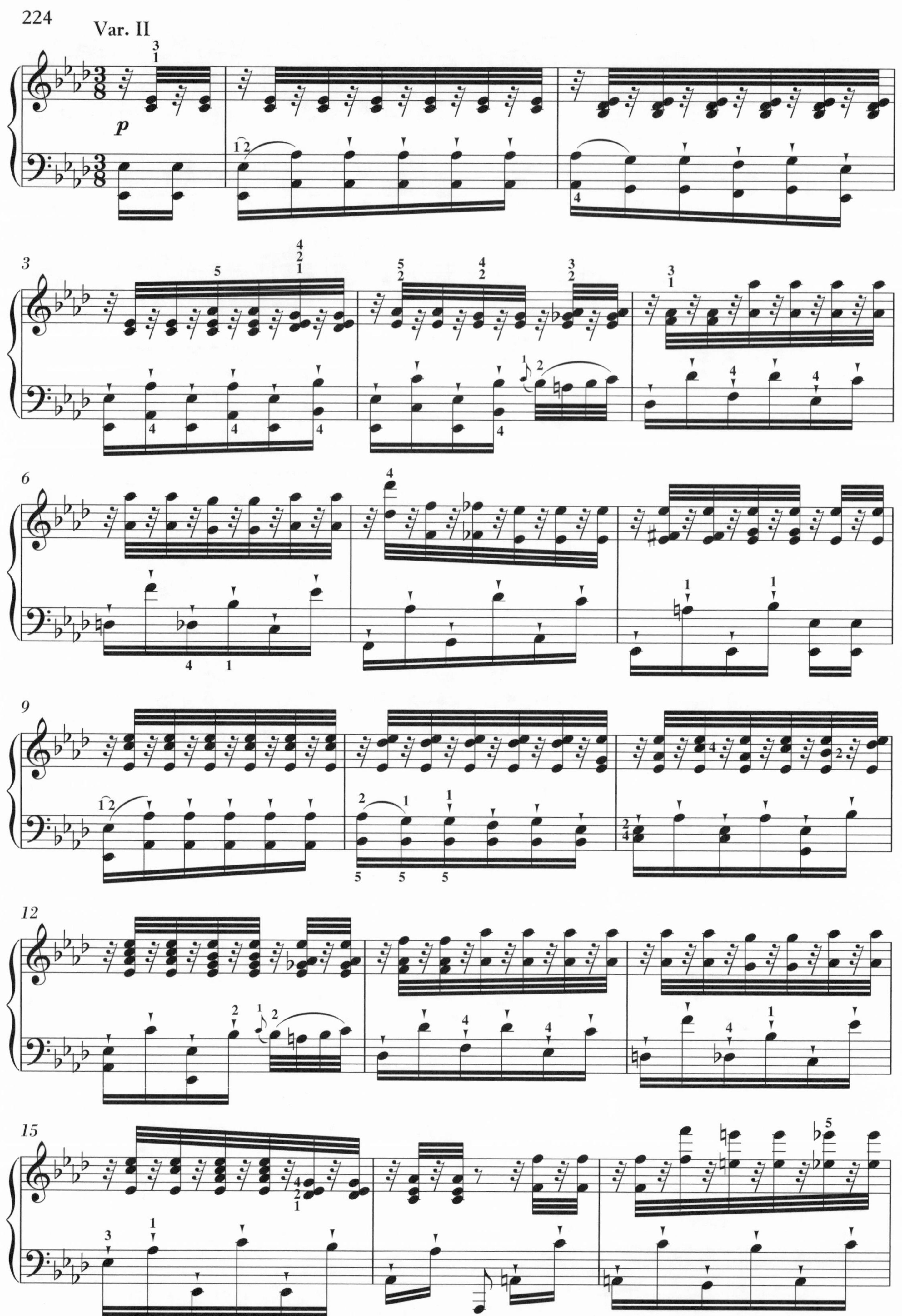

rinf.
p
cresc.
sf
rinf.
p
dim.

d) Thus in the manuscript. Due to a misunderstanding, the first edition (Cappi) has:

Var. IV
pp
sempre staccato
cresc.
sf
pp
sf
sf
sf
sf
sf
sf
sf
decresc.
pp
sf

Var. V
p dolce
cresc.
p
cresc.
p
cresc.

e) without dampers (i.e., with pedal)

SCHERZO La prima parte senza repetizione

Allegro molto (♩. = 76)

f) The natural signs in m. 46 and m. 54 (before the E octave) are not present in the autograph. They are, however, present in the first edition.

g) G in the first edition; G-flat in the autograph score.

MARCIA FUNEBRE sulla morte d'un Eroe (♩ = 60)

h) Note the placement of the "*p*" here on beat four, in contrast to the "*subito p*" on beat one of m. 6.

i) The *cresc*. is placed here in the autograph, making mm. 63-64 intentionally different from mm. 25-26. j) The ♮♭ before the B appears in the first edition, but not in the autograph score.

Allegro (♩ = 126)
p
cresc.
f

sf
p
cre
scen
do
ff
cresc.
sfp

cresc.
f
p
cresc.
f
f
p
cresc.
f
1.
f
p
2.
f
p
f
f
p
f
f
p
f
f
p
f
f
p

cresc.
p
cresc.
f
sf
sf

133
139
cresc.
145
151
cresc.
157
cresc.
163
decresc.
senza sordino

Sonata in E-flat Major

(Sonata quasi una Fantasia)

Opus 27 no. 1
Composed in 1800–01

a) In the first edition (Cappi), the fingering suggestion is 5/3/1.

Copyright © 2010 by G. Schirmer, Inc. (ASCAP) New York, NY
International Copyright Secured. All Rights Reserved

22
pp
26
p
30
cresc.
sf
decresc.
p
34
cresc.
sf
decresc.
p
Allegro (♩. = 88)
36/37
f
p
41
cresc.
p

44/45
48
cresc.
52
56
59
cresc.
Tempo I (♩ = 72)
63

pp
cresc.
sf
decresc.
p
senza sord.
Attacca subito l'Allegro
Allegro molto vivace (♩. = 92)
f
1.
2.

b) without tail

68

1. 2.

p

p

76

85

sempre legato

f

p

p

sempre staccato

94

f

102

p

p

110

cresc.

Attacca subito l'Adagio
Adagio con espressione (♪ = 63)
p
cresc.
fp
sf
decresc.
pp
ff
f

Attacca subito l'Allegro vivace

Allegro vivace (♩ = 120)
cresc.

d) LH over RH e) LH under RH

61
sf
65
sf
70
75
sf
sf
sf
sf
sf
sf
80
sf
tr
p
tr
cresc.
85
f
tr
sf

120
126
131
136
142
149
sf
p
f
ff
fp
pp

157
pp
cresc.
165
cresc.
tr
p
tr
cresc.
171
f
tr
sf
p
sf
176
sf
sf
sf
181
sf
sf
186
sf
sf

191
198
204
209
decresc.
pp
214
cresc.
cresc.
219
f) LH over RH g) LH under RH h) LH over RH

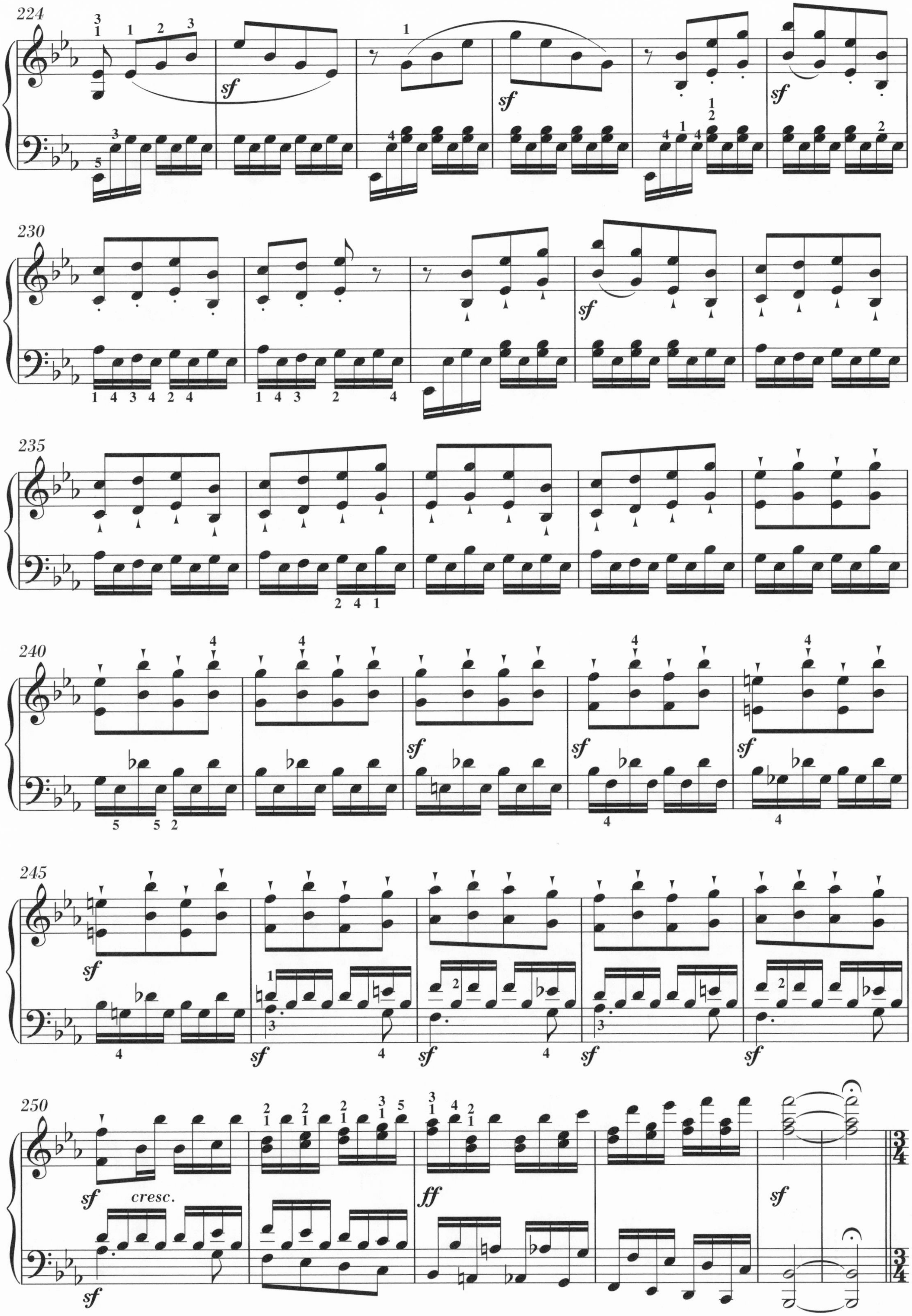
224
sf
230
235
240
245
250
cresc.
ff

256
Adagio
p
cresc.
fp
cresc.
fp
261
cresc.
tr
tr
decresc.
p
sfp
cresc.
tr
264
p
sf
sf
sf
p
attacca
266
Presto
p
sf
sf
274
cresc.
sf
sf
f
280
ff

Dedicated to Countess Giulietta Guicciardi

Sonata in C-sharp minor

(Sonata quasi una Fantasia)

"Moonlight"

Opus 27 no. 2
Composed in 1801

a) The pedal indication (senza sordini—without dampers) is Beethoven's.

Copyright © 2010 by G. Schirmer, Inc. (ASCAP) New York, NY
International Copyright Secured. All Rights Reserved.

40
decresc.
pp
pp

Attacca subito il seguente

Allegretto (♩. = 63)
La prima parte senza repetizione
p
cresc.
sf
p
cresc.
sf
p
Fine
TRIO
sf
sf
sf
sf
sf
sf
fp
fp
pp
fp
fp
cresc.
p–
Allegretto da capo

Presto agitato (𝅗𝅥 = 88)
p
sf
Ped.
cresc.
f

20
p
24
cresc.
28
sf
sf
sf
sf
sf
32
sf
ff
p
35
cresc.
p
ff
p
38
cresc.

f
f
f
f
p
p
cresc.
f
p
cresc.
f
p
cresc. – –
– – decresc.
p

63
cresc.
1.
fp
65b
2.
fp
sf
Ped.
68
sf
Ped.
sf
Ped.
sf
Ped.
71
p
74
77
cresc.
fp

80
83
86
90
97
103
cresc.
cresc.
decresc.
Ped.
Ped.

106
sf
cresc.
sf
Ped. *
Ped. *
109
sf
f
Ped. *
112
116
p
119
cresc.
122
sf
sf

cresc.
cresc.
p cresc.

b) As per autograph score: "normal" pedaling in mm. 163–164; one long pedal in mm. 165–166; "normal" again in m. 167.

165
(ff)
sf
sf
senza sordino
167
p
con sordino
170
p
173
cresc.
177
f
f
180
f

183
186
decresc.
188
Adagio
Tempo I
192
cresc.
195
197

Dedicated to Joseph Edlen von Sonnenfels

Sonata in D Major

Opus 28
Composed in 1801

Allegro (𝅗𝅥. = 66)

15.

a) Fingering in italics and pedal markings are Beethoven's.

Copyright © 2010 by G. Schirmer, Inc. (ASCAP) New York, NY
International Copyright Secured. All Rights Reserved.

b) The autograph does not include ties in the LH in mm. 58–59 nor at the parallel area in the recapitulation mm. 332–333. However, ties are present in both areas in the first edition.

105 *sf* *f* *f* *p*

110

117 *cresc.* *sf* *sf* *sf*

124 *sf* *sf* *sf* *f*

130 *f* *sf* *f* *decresc.* *p*

136

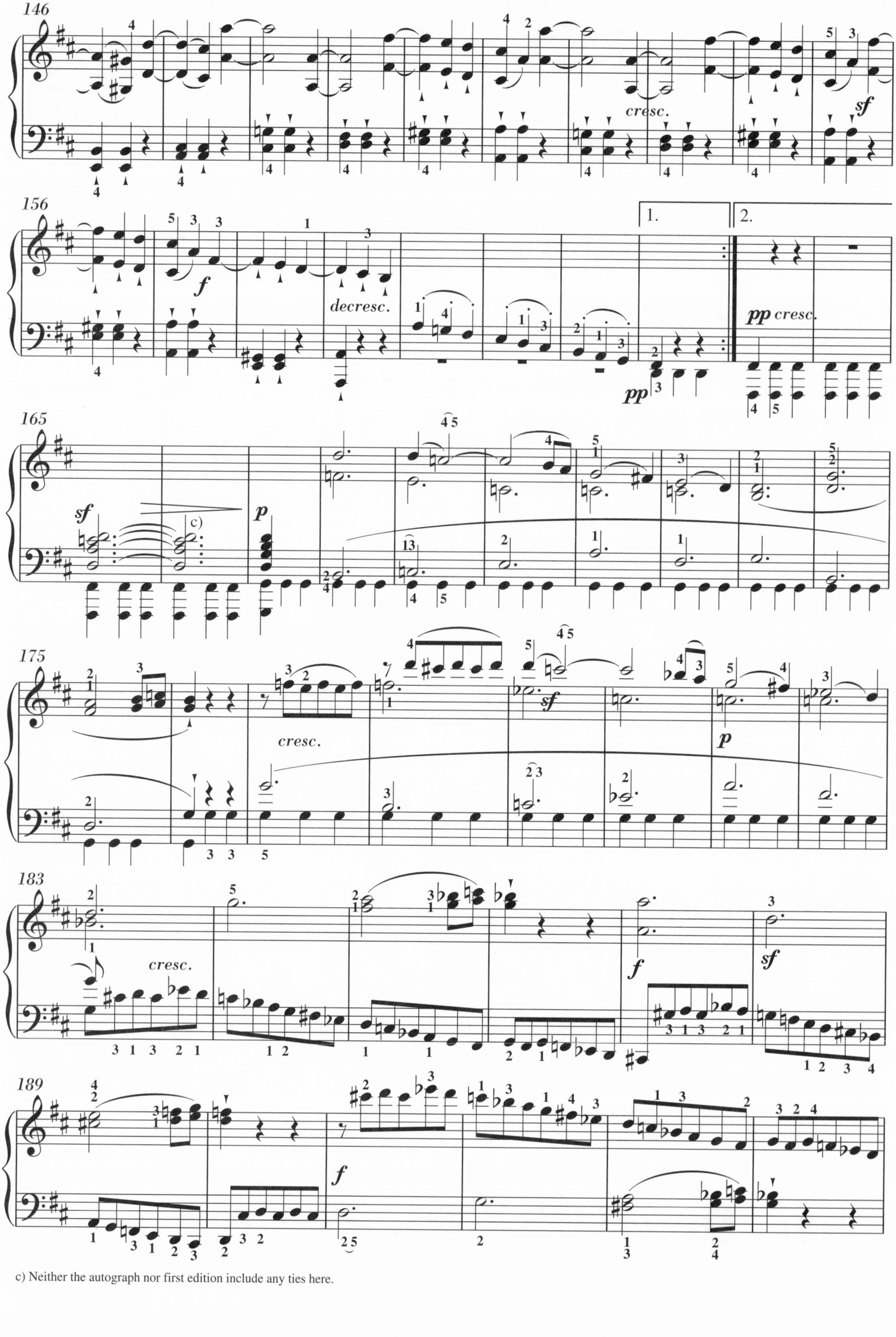
146
cresc.
sf
156
1.
2.
f
decresc.
pp
pp cresc.
165
sf
c)
p
175
cresc.
sf
p
183
cresc.
f
sf
189
f

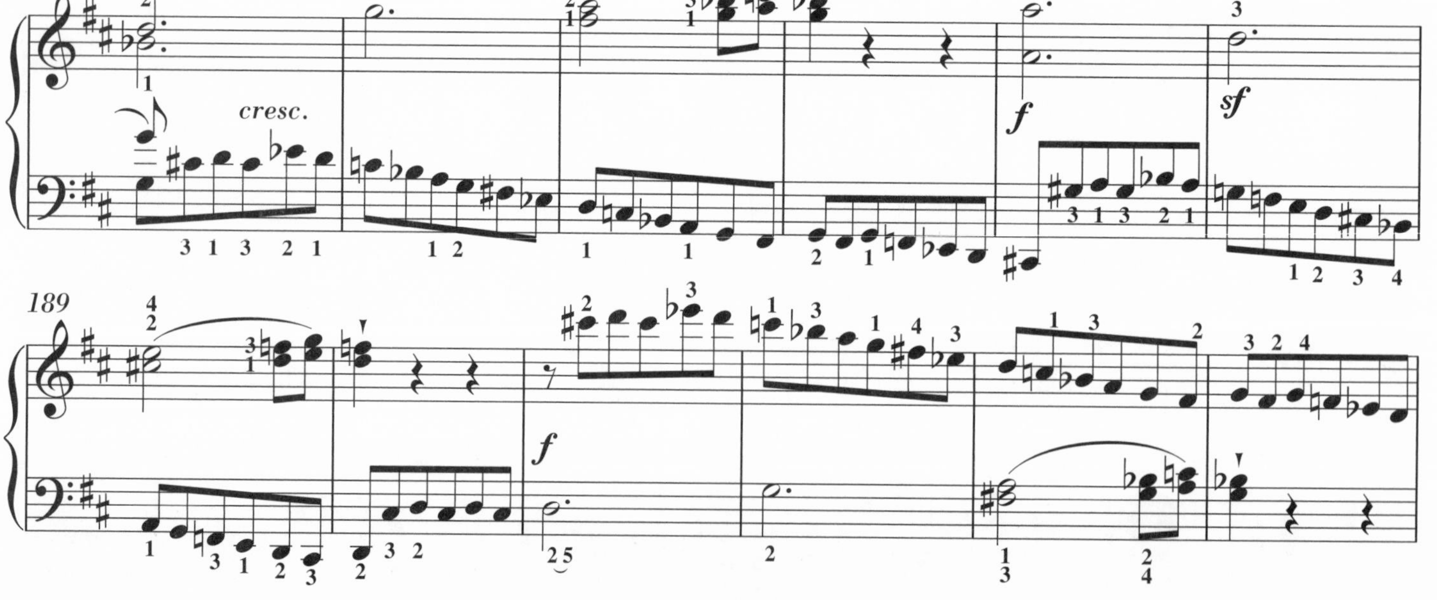

c) Neither the autograph nor first edition include any ties here.

195
201
207
cresc.
213
220
228

cresc.
p
decresc.
Ped.
pp
p
decresc.
Adagio
Tempo I
pp
pp
p
cresc.
sf
(p)

289
cresc.
sf
p
sf
sf
297
sf
p
sf
cresc.
sf
305
p
sf
sf
cresc.
sf
sf
311
fp
fp
fp
321
fp
328
sf
sf
sf
sf
sf
sf
decresc.

335
345
cresc.
353
360
cresc.
367
cresc.
373

379
sf
f
f
383
p
389
cresc.
395
sf
sf
sf
sf
sf
401
sf
sf
f
406
f
sf
decresc.
p

412
421
429
437
445
453
p
cresc.
sf
f
f
decresc.
pp
pp
cresc.
sf
sf
sf
sf
decresc.
p
pp

d) Beethoven's fingerings in the "Andante" and "Rondo" are from the reprinting of these movements in F. Starke's anthology *Viennese Pianoforte School* (1820).

27
decresc.
30a
1.
2.
32
35
38a
1.
2.
cresc.
sempre staccato
42
cresc.
cresc.

47
p
cresc.
50
p
53
cresc.
p
cresc.
p
cresc.
58
p
sf
sf
sf
p
p
64
sf
sf
cresc.
f
p
p
sempre stacc.
70
cresc.

73
sf
sf
sf
cresc.
76
(p)
cresc.
sf
79
sf
sempre legato
cresc.
82
f
p
p
88
p
cresc.
f
p
93
cresc.
sf
sf
p
decresc.
pp
sf
pp

SCHERZO

Allegro vivace (𝅗𝅥. = 92)

e) short appoggiatura

molto legato
cresc.
cresc.
f
p
sf
p
p
sf
sf
sf
sf
sf
f
tr
sf
f
sf

45
sf
sf
49
f
f
p
p
56
62
67
p
73

pp
cresc.
ff
sf

130
molto legato
134
cresc.
138
f
142
p
sf
147
p
151
sf

156
sf
sf
f
sf
sf
tr
162
sf
sf
166
f
f
pp
pp
172
cresc.
p
cresc.
178
f
184

189
p
decresc.
pp
più allegro quasi presto
192
p
cresc.
196
199
f
202
sf
sf
206
sf
ff
ff

ABOUT THE EDITOR

Robert Taub

From New York's Carnegie Hall to Hong Kong's Cultural Centre to Germany's *avant garde* Zentrum für Kunst und Medientechnologie, Robert Taub is acclaimed internationally. He has performed as soloist with the MET Orchestra in Carnegie Hall, the Boston Symphony Orchestra, BBC Philharmonic, The Philadelphia Orchestra, San Francisco Symphony, Los Angeles Philharmonic, Montreal Symphony, Munich Philharmonic, Orchestra of St. Luke's, Hong Kong Philharmonic, Singapore Symphony, and others.

Robert Taub has performed solo recitals on the Great Performers Series at New York's Lincoln Center and other major series worldwide. He has been featured in international festivals, including the Saratoga Festival, the Lichfield Festival in England, San Francisco's Midsummer Mozart Festival, the Geneva International Summer Festival, among others.

Following the conclusion of his highly celebrated New York series of Beethoven Piano Sonatas, Taub completed a sold-out Beethoven cycle in London at Hampton Court Palace. His recordings of the complete Beethoven Piano Sonatas have been praised throughout the world for their insight, freshness, and emotional involvement. In addition to performing, Robert Taub is an eloquent spokesman for music, giving frequent engaging and informal lectures and pre-concert talks. His book on Beethoven—*Playing the Beethoven Piano Sonatas*—has been published internationally by Amadeus Press.

Taub was featured in a recent PBS television program—*Big Ideas*—that highlighted him playing and discussing Beethoven Piano Sonatas. Filmed during his time as Artist-in-Residence at the Institute for Advanced Study, this program has been broadcast throughout the US on PBS affiliates.

Robert Taub's performances are frequently broadcast on radio networks around the world, including the NPR (Performance Today), Ireland's RTE, and Hong Kong's RTHK. He has also recorded the Sonatas of Scriabin and works of Beethoven, Schumann, Liszt, and Babbitt for Harmonia Mundi, several of which have been selected as "critic's favorites" by *Gramophone*, *Newsweek*, *The New York Times*, *The Washington Post*, *Ovation*, and *Fanfare*.

Robert Taub is involved with contemporary music as well as the established literature, premiering piano concertos by Milton Babbitt (MET Orchestra, James Levine) and Mel Powell (Los Angeles Philharmonic), and making the first recordings of the Persichetti Piano Concerto (Philadelphia Orchestra, Charles Dutoit) and Sessions Piano Concerto. He has premiered six works of Milton Babbitt (solo piano, chamber music, Second Piano Concerto). Taub has also collaborated with several 21st-century composers, including Jonathan Dawe (USA), David Bessell (UK), and Ludger Brümmer (Germany) performing their works in America and Europe.

Taub is a Phi Beta Kappa graduate of Princeton where he was a University Scholar. As a Danforth Fellow he completed his doctoral degree at The Juilliard School where he received the highest award in piano. Taub has served as Artist-in-Residence at Harvard University, at UC Davis, as well as at the Institute for Advanced Study. He has led music forums at Oxford and Cambridge Universities and The Juilliard School. Taub has also been Visiting Professor at Princeton University and at Kingston University (UK).